DATE DUE

DEMCO 38-296

GREAT WRITERS OF THE ENGLISH LANGUAGE

Satirists and Humorists

STAFF CREDITS

Executive Editor
Reg Wright

Series Editor
Sue Lyon

Editors
Jude Welton
Sylvia Goulding

Deputy Editors
Alice Peebles
Theresa Donaghey

Features Editors
Geraldine McCaughrean
Emma Foa
Ian Chilvers

Art Editors
Kate Sprawson
Jonathan Alden
Helen James

Designers
Simon Wilder
Frank Landamore

Senior Picture Researchers
Julia Hanson
Vanessa Fletcher
Georgina Barker

Picture Clerk
Vanessa Cawley

Production Controllers
Judy Binning
Tom Helsby

Editorial Secretaries
Fiona Bowser
Sylvia Osborne

Managing Editor
Alan Ross

Editorial Consultant
Maggi McCormick

Publishing Manager
Robert Paulley

Reference Edition Published 1989
Published by Marshall Cavendish Corporation
147 West Merrick Road
Freeport, Long Island
N.Y. 11520

Typeset by Litho Link Ltd., Welshpool
Printed and Bound in Italy by
L.E.G.O. S.p.a. Vicenza

LIBRARY OF CONGRESS
Library of Congress Cataloging-in-Publication Data
Great Writers of the English Language
    p. cm.
    Includes index vol.
    ISBN 1-85435-000-5 (set): $399.95
    1. English literature — History and criticism. 2. English
literature — Stories, plots, etc. 3. American literature — History
and criticism. 4. American literature — Stories, plots, etc.
5. Authors. English — Biography. 6. Authors. American — Biography.
I. Marshall Cavendish Corporation.
PR85.G66 1989
820'.9 – dc19   88-21077
                                                          CIP

ISBN 1–85435–000–5 (set)
ISBN 1–85435–010–2 (vol)

GREAT WRITERS OF THE ENGLISH LANGUAGE

Satirists and Humorists

Jonathan Swift

Lewis Carroll

Evelyn Waugh

Aldous Huxley

MARSHALL CAVENDISH · NEW YORK · TORONTO · LONDON · SYDNEY

CONTENTS

JONATHAN SWIFT

⟨1667-1745⟩

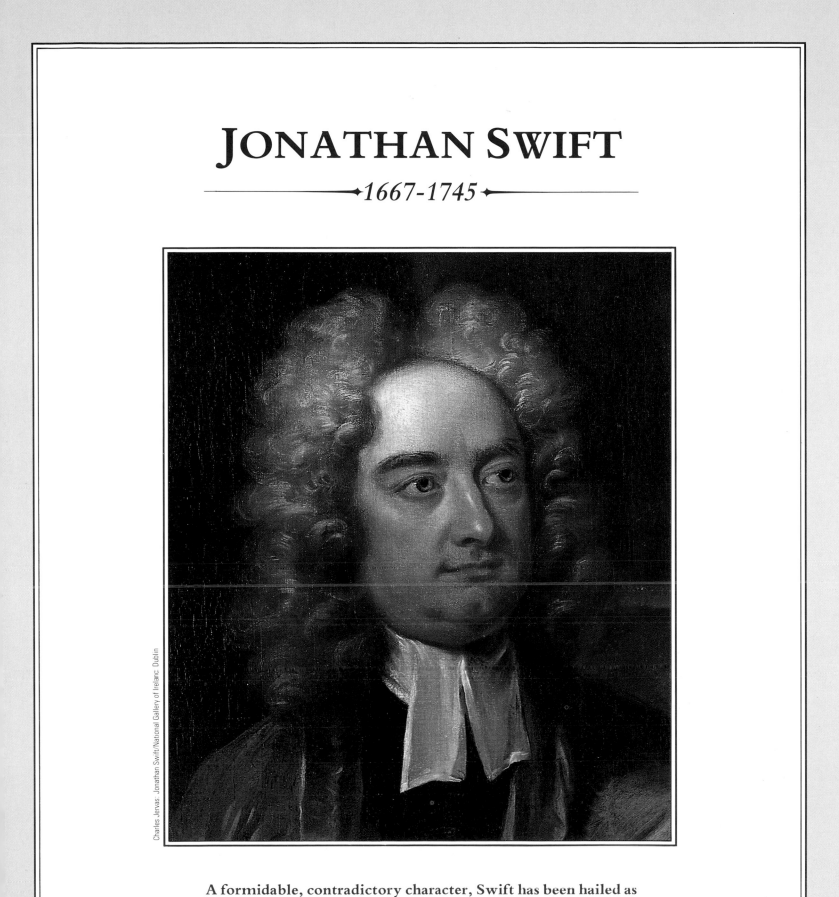

A formidable, contradictory character, Swift has been hailed as
a moralist and satirist of unique power and reviled as a
stunted personality whose genius fed on insecurity and an
inability to love. There is truth in both views of the man who
simultaneously enraged and entertained the society he
lampooned. In his own words, he 'served human liberty', both
as a campaigner for Ireland and through the classic indictment
of political and social corruption, *Gulliver's Travels*.

A Turbulent Priest

One of the most controversial figures of his time, Swift was a clergyman who used the pen rather than the pulpit to blaze forth his passionate denunciations of contemporary society.

Just as the miniature inhabitants of Lilliput pulled down the 'giant' Gulliver, so history has dealt with Jonathan Swift. *Gulliver's Travels*, the most savage satire ever written on human society, is now widely read as a children's tale, while its brilliant author is often thought of merely as a children's writer – and a peculiar one at that. The truth is that, despite constant ill health, Swift fought from strength, not weakness, and won immortality among the foremost satirical geniuses of all time. He also ranks as a notable poet, political activist and supporter of the poor.

Jonathan Swift was born of impoverished English parents in Hoey's Court, Dublin, on 30 November 1667. His mother, Abigail Erick or Herrick, came from a respectable Leicester family and was distantly related to the poet Robert Herrick. Swift's father, also named Jonathan, was descended from an old Yorkshire family which suffered badly during the Civil War, his own father having been dispossessed of all he owned and never compensated.

The senior Jonathan Swift became a steward, or domestic manager, to a barristers' chambers in the capital – a respectable position but one which was tragically short-lived. He died suddenly several months before the birth of his only son, leaving his young wife with an 18-month-old daughter and very little money.

CHILDHOOD ABDUCTION

While still a baby, Jonathan was abducted. It transpired later that the nurse looking after him had taken him with her to a gravely ill relative in Whitehaven, Cumberland – and just stayed. It took nearly three years for Mrs Swift to track them down, during which time she suffered much anguish, only partially abated when she learned that her baby had been taken across the Irish Sea (her sister-in-law and nephew perished on one such crossing). Mrs Swift ordered the nurse not to risk the return voyage until Jonathan was 'better able to bear it'. In her defence, it can be said that the nurse, who adored him, took excellent care of

Insecure childhood
Swift was born in the house above in Dublin. Fatherless at birth, he saw little of his mother, and at the age of six was sent to school in Kilkenny (below left). Lack of parental affection left him insecure.

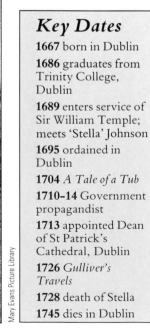

Key Dates

1667 born in Dublin

1686 graduates from Trinity College, Dublin

1689 enters service of Sir William Temple; meets 'Stella' Johnson

1695 ordained in Dublin

1704 *A Tale of a Tub*

1710–14 Government propagandist

1713 appointed Dean of St Patrick's Cathedral, Dublin

1726 *Gulliver's Travels*

1728 death of Stella

1745 dies in Dublin

Trinity College, Dublin
Swift spent four years at Ireland's most prestigious seat of learning (left), but his real education came later in years of private reading.

the boy; by the age of three, so the story goes, young Jonathan Swift could read the Bible.

When he was six, Jonathan was sent to Kilkenny College, the leading Anglican school in Ireland. For eight years, his intellectual precocity was developed through a rigorous, classical education. He later recalled it as a period of happiness unaffected by 'the confinement ten hours a day to nouns and verbs, the terror of the rod, the bloody noses and broken shins'.

In fact, the young Swift was moody, self-dramatizing, given to extremes of exultation and despair – all stemming from a sense of neglect. For this, he blamed all his adult relatives – unfairly, since, with the exception of his mother, who preferred her daughter, they did their best for him.

His moodiness is apparent in a portrait painted when he was about 14 and just starting as a student at Trinity College, Dublin (the Swifts could not afford Oxford, his first choice); his full mouth looks set, his gaze fiercely intelligent yet mocking.

A BOISTEROUS STUDENT

Swift was an average, high-spirited undergraduate. He missed lectures, neglected his studies, was accused of starting 'tumults', and gained his degree at 18 only by special dispensation. Career choices in those days were limited, and personal progress often depended on finding a generous or influential patron. Swift was invited to enter the service of retired diplomat Sir William Temple – a relative-by-marriage of his mother's – as his private secretary/bookkeeper at £20 a year plus full board. If the rewards were modest, Swift's duties at Sir William's fine Surrey mansion – Moor Park, near Farnham – were far from onerous.

In his small room on the ground floor, Swift had up to eight hours daily to indulge his passion for reading, and apparently amassed enough books during his years there to last a lifetime. He was able to study for his Master's degree – a qualification for entering the Church, which was a possibility for his future career. And there was time to write. His early verse efforts earned a crushing snub from his relative, the famous poet-

Wayward scholar
(right) This portrait shows Swift at 14, soon after he became an undergraduate. He often abandoned lectures in favour of 'frequenting the town'.

Distinguished patron
After university, Swift entered the household of Sir William Temple (below), a distinguished retired diplomat, at his home, Moor Park in Surrey (bottom).

playwright John Dryden: 'Cousin Swift, you will never be a poet' – a comment for which Jonathan never forgave him. But Sir William, who was both employer and a surrogate father, encouraged him, sharing the youth's idealism and nurturing his growing interest in politics.

The atmosphere at Moor Park proved both relaxing and stimulating – an ideal hothouse for completing Swift's education. As his intellectual

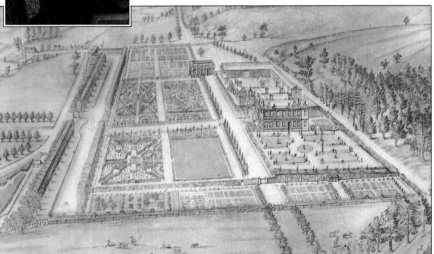

7

horizon broadened, so his confidence grew. Any assumption that Swift's fiercely independent and moral outlook made him uncomfortable to be with is only half the truth. Certainly he could be arrogant and formidable – but only in the face of stupidity and hypocrisy. He was friendly to straightforward, unpretentious people, charming and witty in good company – particularly that of attractive young women – and fond of walking, swimming and card games.

It was at Moor Park that symptoms first emerged of Swift's lifelong illness, now thought to have been Ménière's disease (excess fluid in the inner ear, causing giddiness and deafness). And there also he first met a little raven-haired girl called Esther Johnson, whom he renamed 'Stella' and to whom he later addressed his celebrated *Journal to Stella*. She was eight years old and doted on by Sir William, who had virtually adopted her after the death of her father, his steward.

A BLAZING ROW

After nearly five years at Moor Park, Swift felt restless for wider achievement. He waited impatiently for the help his mentor had promised, and at last there was a blazing row – Swift determined to take holy orders, and the old man was desperate to retain his indispensable services. In January 1695, Swift was ordained in Dublin, and appointed prebendary priest to the small lonely parish of Kilroot, near Belfast, at an annual stipend of £100.

The following year, he returned to Moor Park at Sir William's invitation, remaining there until the latter's death in 1699. Swift devoted his considerable energies to editing the old man's papers and penning the satirical masterpiece *A Tale of a Tub*. The book appeared in 1704 and was an instant sell-out. By then, the author was back in Ireland, first as chaplain to the Earl of Berkeley and later as the £250-a-year vicar of Laracor, close

'Most valuable friend'
(above left) Swift was devoted to Esther Johnson (whom he renamed Stella) from her childhood days.

The lure of London
(above) Swift regarded himself as essentially English and was at home in London's literary and political circles.

Cantankerous friend
(right) Alexander Pope,
one of the outstanding
poets of the 18th century,
was among Swift's best
friends in the literary
world. His body was
stunted by illness and he
was notoriously
quarrelsome and spiteful,
but he was generous to his
friends, and Swift said he
had 'fifty times more
charity for mankind than
I could ever pretend to'.

Teeming humanity
(below) Swift was
ambivalent in his attitudes
towards his fellow men
and women. He cared
intensely about
individuals and was
charitable to the poor, but
he often felt disgust at the
masses.

ary collaborator, Joseph Addison. Both men were
to become close friends of Swift, until political differences intervened. They formed a threesome
who nevertheless often met up in pairs, never
needing, as Swift commented, 'a third person, to
support or enliven [our] conversation'.

Although Swift shared his friends' Whig (early
Liberal) convictions, he was appalled when the
party supported Dissenters in Ireland. In 1710, he
joined the newly elected Tories and, at the express
wish of their leader, Robert Harley, later Earl of
Oxford, became the Government's chief political
writer. This shift necessitated a move away from
Addison and Steele, causing considerable sadness:

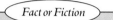

Fact or Fiction

SATIRIZING SCIENCE

S wift hated the abstraction and aridity
of science, and through Gulliver he
derides Europe's oldest scientific institu-
tion, the Royal Society. The academics of
Lagado are engaged on such absurd pro-
jects as the extraction of sunbeams from
cucumbers, but Swift's satire contains as
much fact as exaggeration.

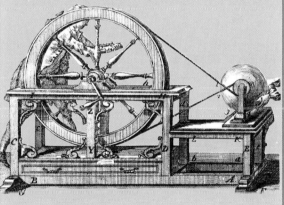

to Dublin. Stella, now grown to mature beauty,
followed with her companion, Rebecca Dingley.
A Tale of a Tub was published anonymously, like
many of Swift's works, but suspicions were
enough; his Church career was blighted perpetually by the ironic aspersions against Christianity in
this and later books.

CHAMPION OF THE POOR
"Had he but spared his tongue and pen/he might
have rose like other men", Swift wrote of himself
in due course. That he continued to expect promo-
tion is one of the numerous contradictions in
his complex character. Passionate but iron-
controlled, he liked women yet was repelled by
female sexuality; he despised extravagance but
spent freely on good food and drink; he lived
healthily yet had a morbid interest in sewage; he
was occasionally snobbish and self-pitying yet
constantly generous – at least one-third of his
income went to the poor of Ireland. He saved
probably hundreds from starving to death.

Such contrasts are not unknown in clever but
repressed people. With Swift, they were facets of
his personality, not the substance. More significant was his absorption in affairs of state. By 1707,
he was an envoy of the Irish Church, in close
contact with Court and Government circles in
London. If his intellectual opinions shook the
Establishment, his basic loyalty and negotiating
skill went unquestioned.

Swift's writings, which included political
essays, pamphlets and miscellaneous verse
brought him many new admirers. Among them
was the coterie of authors presided over by
Richard Steele, editor of *The Tatler*, and his liter-

'Mr Addison and I are different as black and
white', Swift wrote in his *Journal*, 'and I believe our
friendship will go off, by this damned business of
party; he cannot bear seeing me fall in so with the
ministry; but I love him still as well as ever . . .'

As a leading political writer, Swift's two main
achievements were to add his voice, successfully,
to ending the 21-year-war with France, and to persuade the Tories that the correct power-balance
between monarch, Lords and Commons was vital
for stable democracy. This was a tenet which he
expounded in weekly articles for the *Examiner* between November 1710 and June 1711.

This period was momentous for Swift in other
ways – "plaguy busy", as he confided to the *Journal* one "vengeance cold" night at his three-room
lodgings in Bury Street, off London's elegant Pic-
cadilly. His mother, whom he had visited and supported over the years, died in April 1710. But
more happily, he was developing "a mighty
friendship" with Esther (or Hester) Vanhomrigh,

the eldest daughter of an Anglo-Dutch merchant and former Lord Mayor (her mother was Swift's landlady). Twenty-two years old, strong-featured and direct, Esther fell hopelessly in love with Swift. Although partly detailed in his poem *Cadenus and Vanessa* (his pseudonyms for the two of them), the full extent of their relationship remains unknown. Yet she pursued him so

relentlessly and with such jealousy of his cherished Stella that Swift finally ended their association. 'Vanessa' died broken-hearted in June 1723.

Meanwhile, Swift's reward for political services was not the English bishopric he had hoped for, but elevation as Dean of St Patrick's Cathedral, Dublin, in April 1713. Sick with his recurrent ailment – "I have the noise of seven watermills in my ears" – he accepted with bad grace the appointment he felt he had been "thrown into". His spirits sank lower still when the Tories fell in 1714.

'SEDITIOUS LIBEL'

Any expectation of further advancement was finished. From now on, Swift centred his attention on St Patrick's, becoming not only an excellent manager of cathedral revenues but a very popular preacher of "plain, honest stuff". He set up a loan fund for tradesmen and urged a boycott of English goods to protect Irish jobs. He proposed agricultural improvements and opposed the planned National Bank and new coinage as potentially exploitative.

Furious at the poverty around him, Swift tried to shock people into action against the conditions that produced it. He suggested, for example, that the population be controlled by eating children. Under the guise of a fictional clothier in his *Drapier's Letters* (1724), he counselled the Irish to employ first passive resistance and then open defiance against English imperialism. A Government charge against the publisher of 'scandalous, seditious libel' collapsed when the jury refused eight times to return a 'guilty' verdict.

A subsequent bid to silence the Dean was dropped after chief minister Walpole was warned that his arrest could not be safely made with fewer than 10,000 troops. Although Swift loathed so-

Delville Gardens
(above) Swift was an austere man in many ways, but he loved gardens. This one, a few miles from Dublin, was a particular favourite and he often visited it.

Friend or lover?
Esther Vanhomrigh (above) – Swift's 'Vanessa' – came into his life during his stay in London in 1707-09. She was in love with him, but he probably regarded her more as a surrogate daughter, and it is not known whether their relationship ever became physical.

Dublin's fair city
When Swift was born, Dublin was still essentially medieval in aspect, but during the 18th century it was largely rebuilt as a handsome classical city.

A View of the City of Dublin from the Magazine Hill in the Phœnix Park.

Mary Delany: The Beggars' Hut in the Gardens of Delville, Dublin/National Gallery of Ireland

THE BEGGAR'S OPERA

'What think you of a Newgate pastoral, among the whores and thieves there?' With this throwaway line Swift inspired his friend John Gay to create one of the most famous musical dramas of the 18th century – *The Beggar's Opera*. Set in London's most infamous prison, it featured memorable low-life characters and ridiculed Sir Robert Walpole's Whig administration. The show opened in London on 29 January 1728 to instant popular acclaim.

Hogarth: Scene from the 'Beggar's Opera'/Tate Gallery, London

called 'ordinary people', portraying them as the idle, greedy and repulsive 'Yahoos' in his most famous book, they for their part adored him. *Gulliver's Travels* may have germinated within the ranks of the Scriblerus Club. This was an association of writers formed in 1714 by Swift and his friend John Arbuthnot, including such notables as the poet Alexander Pope and playwright John Gay. Together these men playfully decided to create the memoirs of their imaginary founder, Martin Scriblerus, and wrote a number of major works during this fertile fellowship.

Gulliver's Travels took Swift four years to write.

James Malton: St Patrick's Cathedral, Dublin/National Gallery of Ireland

St Patrick's Cathedral (below) Swift became Dean here in 1713. The dean is the chief administrator of a cathedral, and Swift performed his duties conscientiously. He is buried in the cathedral.

He brought the manuscript to London in March 1726 and, calling himself 'Richard Sympson' for safety, arranged its publication in return for £200. Fearing prosecution, publisher Benjamin Motte toned down parts of the text without reference to its author.

Swift's bitterness about Motte's amendments was tempered by the book's resounding success immediately it appeared on 28 October that year. Arbuthnot related that it was 'in everybody's hands'. Politicians thought the satire 'too severe', churchmen that its aim was 'impious'. Swift had succeeded in both vexing and diverting the world. The first printing sold out in a week.

A SECRET MARRIAGE?

Stella, his 'most valuable' friend, died in January 1728, after a long and painful illness. Reports that she and Swift were married during her last days remain unproved. He consoled himself with more writing, further charitable acts, and visits to his many friends. 'Life is good for nothing', he wrote to Pope, 'otherwise than for the love we have to our friends.'

Swift suffered a stroke in 1742 and died on 19 October 1745, aged 77. He was buried in St Patrick's Cathedral, close to Stella's final resting place, and left the bulk of his fortune to endow a mental hospital.

GULLIVER'S TRAVELS

Combining the fascination of an adventure story with the bite of satire, *Gulliver's Travels* has never ceased to appeal to people of all ages, from 'the cabinet council to the nursery'.

Written as a satirical comedy, *Gulliver's Travels* was intended "to vex the world rather than divert it". Swift certainly succeeded in vexing the Victorians, particularly Thackeray, who found the last voyage in the book "filthy in word, filthy in thought, furious, raging, obscene."

For contemporary readers, *Gulliver's Travels* remains a fascinating allegorical tale of one man's mental and spiritual journey as he voyages to strange far-flung lands. On his travels he encounters bizarre creatures who, on closer observation, are perhaps not that different from himself.

GUIDE TO THE PLOT

The hero, Lemuel Gulliver, is a ship's surgeon who in the first part is shipwrecked on the island of Lilliput, where he finds a replica of human society in miniature. Gulliver is tied up by hundreds of tiny human creatures and ingeniously conveyed to the capital city to meet the Emperor.

Fascinated by the "Man-Mountain", the little people flock to view Gulliver, while the Emperor and ministers of state concern themselves with how to feed and care for such a giant. They grant him his liberty, dependent on various conditions. And in response to an appeal from the Emperor, he agrees to help the Lilliputians fight their enemies on the island of Blefuscu, who are amassing their fleet for an invasion.

Gulliver wades across to Blefuscu and pulls the enemy fleet ashore to Lilliput, so putting an end to the threatened invasion and gaining honours for himself among the Lilliputians. But the Emperor wants more assistance from Gulliver to make the whole of Blefuscu subject to Lilliput rule. Gulliver's refusal to be "an instrument of bringing a free and brave people into slavery" casts him into disfavour. When he learns of his impending charge, he leaves for Blefuscu and eventually returns home to his wife and family.

A Voyage to Brobdingnag forms the second part of Gulliver's adventures. This time, he finds himself in a land peopled by giants, where even rats, wasps and dogs are of frightening proportions. Taken in by a farmer, Gulliver is made to work for his board by travelling to market towns and performing all day for an incredulous audience. He is tenderly cared for by nine-year-old Glumdalclitch, the farmer's daughter, who stays with Gulliver when

> "*I felt something alive moving on my left leg, which advancing gently forward over my breast, came almost up to my chin . . . I perceived it to be a tiny human creature not six inches high, with a bow and arrow in his hands, and a quiver at his back.*"

he is sold to the Queen for a thousand gold pieces.

A special little bed-chamber is made for Gulliver where he can be safe from most hazards, although he suffers several accidents which alarm Glumdalclitch and make Gulliver feel both frightened and

In Lilliput
(right) Prisoner of the tiny, intrepid Lilliputians, the 'gigantic' Gulliver secretly admires their daring "to walk and mount on my body while one of my hands was at liberty". With much ingenuity, they bear him off to their capital where he meets his Majesty, the Emperor.

Court frolics
(below) Peering through a window in the Palace, Gulliver observes how the distinguished few win the Emperor's favours – by alternately "leaping and creeping" over an extended stick.

Willy Pogány, Gulliver's Travels/©Harrap Ltd/Mary Evans Picture Library

Mansell Collection

In Brobdingnag
In this land of giants, Gulliver finds he is of Lilliputian size. While he is treated with great consideration by the King (above) and Queen, his littleness exposes him to all kinds of accidents. He is pelted with apples by the Queen's jealous dwarf (left) and, finally, is carried off in his travelling-box by a passing eagle (right).

have no time for practicalities such as building good houses.

Gulliver tires of being confined to the King's floating island and is dropped down to Balnibarbi, where he is shown wild schemes devised by professors in the Academy of Projectors, while all around the land lies wasted and people starve. Gulliver moves on to Glubbdubdrib, the Island of Sorcerers, where he calls up his favourite heroes from the dead. On another island called Luggnagg, he is enraptured to hear of a race of immortals, but they prove to be a horrifying vision of everlasting senility.

A Voyage to the Houyhnhnms is Gulliver's last adventure. The victim of a mutiny, he is set ashore on a strange land where he encounters the Yahoos, a disgusting species of animal which bears a frightening resemblance to the human form. The land is populated by the Houyhnhnms, a noble race of horses who gradually appear to Gulliver to be "the perfection of nature". Gulliver tries to explain his own world, but is met with perplexity, for the Houyhnhnms have no language for lying, treachery and evil. They can only believe Gulliver has said

ridiculous. He spends many hours with the King, who is curious to discover more about the lifestyle and government of Gulliver's homeland. The more the King learns, the more horrified he becomes. Gulliver considers the King politically naïve, but is nevertheless discomfited by his damning pronouncement on the human race.

The third of Gulliver's travels takes him eastward to Laputa, a mysterious flying island inhabited by strange people lost in "intense speculations". Interested only in music and mathematics, the Laputians

"the thing which is not". Gulliver hopes for nothing more than to spend his life among the gentle Houyhnhnms, whom he has learnt to love and respect, but his journeys are not yet over . . .

SATIRE AND ALLEGORY
Gulliver's Travels is primarily a satire on the politics of Swift's era. It is also a novel concerned with the hero's variety of experiences and his consequent development. Filled with contemporary political references – which may strike a chord in substance if not in detail – the book is as

vivid and alive as ever, thanks to Swift's comic artistry and his timeless theme of human corruption. The book is not so much a critique of humanity as a whole as an attack on those who abuse their positions of power and influence. Swift hated institutions but loved the individual: "I hate and detest that animal called man, although I heartily love John, Peter, Thomas, and so forth."

The individual in *Gulliver's Travels* is Gulliver himself. His careful and methodical account of the different worlds he explores forms the basis of the story. Of greater significance is his place as a human being in each of these worlds. In this sense Gulliver is an allegorical figure; his experiences encompass the human experience and what he observes has meaning for all of us. The irony of the tale lies in Gulliver's inability to recognize the wider significance of his various encounters. Swift uses him as a device to expose the political cruelty and corruption of 18th-century society.

A MINIATURE STATE

The story of Gulliver's adventures in Lilliput is easily the most delightful of the four journeys. The detail and wit describing Gulliver's stay among the tiny Lilliputians have made this section an enduring children's classic. *A Voyage to Lilliput* is also a political history incorporating the

Mary Evans Picture Library

> ". . . he looked upon us as a sort of animals to whose share . . . some small pittance of reason had fallen, whereof we made no other use than by its assistance to aggravate our natural corruptions, and to acquire new ones which nature had not given us."

Cobweb research
(above) Gulliver visits the Academy of Lagado, where one scientist is busy trying to make silk from spiders' webs, and tint it by feeding the spiders on a diet of flies "most beautifully coloured".

Arthur Rackham: A Laputan Gentleman taking a walk/With permission of Barbara Edwards, daughter of the artist

A weird people
On the island of Laputa, Gulliver meets the learned but vague inhabitants (left), who are totally engrossed in music and mathematics, while lacking all "imagination, fancy, and invention". When they go out, they are attended by servants who attract their attention with a "flapper" – a kind of rattle. Without the aid of this warning device they would be "in manifest danger of falling down every precipice . . ."

reigns of Queen Anne and King George I and the rocky careers of several leading statesmen. Gulliver's observation of the Emperor's ingratitude is a direct comment on King George's greed:

"Of so little weight are the greatest services to princes, when put in the balance with a refusal to gratify their passions." Gulliver as a giant is the moral superior of the Lilliputians. In his voyage to Brobdingnag, the situation is reversed.

The King of Brobdingnag is very much Swift's ideal monarch. He spends many hours extracting the truth from Gulliver about the history and culture of Europe, and can only conclude that Gulliver's fellow humans must be "the most pernicious race of little odious vermin that Nature ever suffered to crawl upon the surface of the earth." Gulliver offers the formula for gunpowder to the King and only makes matters worse. The King expresses horror

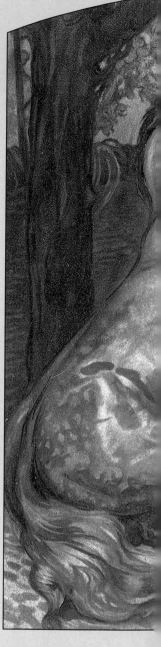

Gulliver's story
(above) Becoming proficient in the Houyhnhnm language, Gulliver converses with the master, who is curious about his origins. Gulliver tells him about life in Europe much of which the master finds difficult to grasp because he has no knowledge of power, war, law, money or treachery. He concludes that Gulliver is closer to the bestial Yahoos (right) than his own noble race.

at the thought of so much deliberate destruction and suggests that:

"whoever could make two ears of corn, or two blades of grass to grow upon a spot of ground where only one grew before, would . . . do more essential service to his country, than the whole race of politicians put together."

Brobdingnag with its stable system of government and benign ruler is a Utopian state which England would do well to imitate. Book Three of Gulliver's voyages contrasts sharply with this ideal. The state of affairs in Laputa and Balnibarbi is so dreadful as to serve as an allegory of the worst excesses of 18th-century folly and corruption. Gulliver becomes a shadowy figure in this section, as Swift's denunciation of bad government and wild schemes comes to the fore.

BESTIAL HUMANITY

In the final book, Gulliver receives his biggest surprise. He has stumbled into a society of truly rational beings whose existence reduces him to the level of animal. It is a stroke of Swift's brilliance that he elevates animals to fill the place which humans believe is rightfully theirs. The Houyhnhnms are horses and at the same time perfect creatures of order, while the human Yahoos are filthy creatures of instinct. The allegory of man's essential baseness and amorality is complete. Gulliver becomes unable to say *"the thing which is not"* and virtually incapable of living among his own kind again.

One of Swift's most important arguments in *Gulliver's Travels* is that human beings are capable of reason but that this does not therefore mean that they are rational. The book is filled with descriptions of human degeneracy and abuses of the power of reason.

The wonderful world of Lilliput is simply a microcosm of society, and is riddled with just the same vices. Brobdingnag has its fair share of ugliness, and is simply the human condition magnified. The islands of the third book are steeped in an atmosphere of dereliction and death, the result of wilfully misguided human endeavour.

It is in describing the Houyhnhnms that Swift's point is made most forcibly. The Yahoos possess no power of reason – they are simply bestial and therefore not culpable. Houyhnhnms on the other hand "are endowed by nature with a general disposition to all virtues". Somewhere in between is Gulliver. His explanation of the causes and art of war at home confirms the Houyhnhnm master in his belief that Gulliver and his people "instead of Reason . . . were only possessed of some quality fitted to increase our natural vices . . ."

Gulliver is forced to accept that he is a Yahoo after all. He differs from them only in wearing clothes and possessing a thin veneer of civilization. The ability to reason, which is supposedly the crucial difference between humans and animals, is not enough to keep him from vice.

In the Background

INTO THE UNKNOWN

Voyages to distant lands were one of the hallmarks of Queen Anne's reign, and William Dampier (right) was the most intrepid English traveller of the period. He had a remarkable career at sea as sailor, pirate and navigator. He travelled to the East Indies, the north coast of Australia and the Pacific, and completed two round-the-world voyages. He wrote up his travels in a vigorous, factual style, and his chief work, *A Voyage Round the World*, appeared in 1697. Such books were extremely popular and this particular travelogue provided a direct inspiration for *Gulliver's Travels*. Swift-as-Gulliver refers to it in his introductory letter, even pretending that Dampier is his cousin.

CHARACTERS IN FOCUS

The characters in *Gulliver's Travels* are as extreme and varied as the countries. Inherently comic creations; they are often also contemporary kings or politicians in satiric disguise. The Emperor of Lilliput is modelled on George I, and his treacherous minister Flimnap on the statesman Sir Robert Walpole. As the characters increase in size, they lose their charm but retain the most absurd and vicious attributes of human nature.

WHO'S WHO

Gulliver The dauntless hero, whose spirit of adventure and fascination with other cultures take him to extraordinary lands.

The Emperor of Lilliput The "Delight and Terror of the Universe", liberal with Gulliver, belligerent towards his neighbours.

Flimnap The scheming treasurer of Lilliput, who hates Gulliver.

The King of Brobdingnag The benign and wise monarch of the land of giants, who is "perfectly astonished" by Gulliver's account of European affairs.

Glumdal-clitch A nine-year-old Brobdingnagian girl who loves and cares for Gulliver, her "manikin".

The Court of Laputa The crazed aristocracy of a flying island, who are "so taken up with intense speculations" that they neglect their people.

The Struld-bruggs Immortal beings condemned to perpetual senility in the land of Luggnagg.

The Houy-hnhnms A noble, rational race of horses, whose chief virtues are "friendship and benevolence".

The Yahoos Hairy, naked humanoids, as backward and "disagreeable" as the Houyhnhnms are gentle and enlightened.

Don Pedro A Portuguese ship's captain, who treats Gulliver with kindness.

Mary Evans Picture Library

Gulliver's "little nurse" in Brobdingnag, Glumdalclitch (below) is his champion and protectress. "She was very good-natured and not above forty foot high, being little for her age" Gulliver recalls, saying, "to her I chiefly owe my preservation in that country." Mishaps befall him only when he is away from her care.

Mary Evans Picture Library

Astute and adaptable, Gulliver (above) can be reassuring or resilient, according to the size and demeanour of the people he meets. He endears himself to the Lilliputians by his "gentleness and good behaviour".

As active and inquisitive as they are minute, the Lilliputians (right) search the pockets of "the Great Man-Mountain". His watch is borne off by "two of [the] tallest Yeomen of the Guards" – they take it to be his "god", for he tells them "he seldom did anything without consulting it".

Mansell Collection

The noblest creatures that Gulliver meets are the Houyhnhnms (right) – a word signifying "the perfection of nature". These horses have an ordered society, free of vice, light years away from the corruption and misery permeating humankind. In their midst, Gulliver's values alter radically and he asks, "who can read of the virtues I have mentioned in the glorious Houyhnhnms, without being ashamed of his own vices, when he considers himself as the reasoning, governing animal of his country?"

Mansell Collection

The King of Brobdingnag (above) is a "Prince of excellent understanding", with whom Gulliver has frequent conversations about English "wars by sea and land . . . schisms in religion, and parties in the state", all of which give the King a poor view of such "diminutive insects" as Europeans. Gulliver is at first thrown into a patriotic fury, but later concedes there might be some justice in the King's opinion. Accordingly, his sense of national and personal pride shrinks – "I really began to imagine myself dwindled many degrees below my usual size."

"A very courteous and generous person", **Don Pedro** (right) bears the brunt of Gulliver's fear and loathing of his fellow 'Yahoos'. Gulliver records that he was "ready to faint at the very smell of him and his men", and it is only through Don Pedro's perseverance and sensitivity that Gulliver begins "to tolerate his company".

Fotomas

Christie's London/Bridgeman Art Library

SAVAGE INDIGNATION

Abrasive and unstinting in his exposure of human injustice, Swift was inspired by a 'savage indignation' – his self-decreed epitaph – to challenge, shock and, ultimately, 'mend the world'.

Charles Jervas: Jonathan Swift/National Portrait Gallery, London

After Lely: Duchess of Somerset/National Portrait Gallery, London

'A conjured spirit'
Resentment, outrage, frustration and a wicked sense of humour drove Jonathan Swift (left) to write some foolish, some insulting, some brilliant and some profoundly wise works. Anonymity and a variety of pseudonyms did not keep his readers from recognizing his distinctive authorship.

Fiery 'carrots'
The Countess of Somerset (right) was one powerful member of the aristocracy whom Swift alienated with an impudent verse, in which he mocked her, red hair and all.

Jonathan Swift seems to have been a compulsive writer. As a young man of 22 he told a cousin that 'There is something in me which must be employed, and when I am alone, turns all, for want of practice, into speculation and thought; insomuch that in these seven weeks I have been here, I have writ and burnt, and writ again, upon almost all manner of subjects more perhaps than any man in England.' His mind was 'like a conjured spirit, that would do mischief if I would not give it employment'.

It was also teeming with the ideas, images, associations, puns and jokes that made Swift such wonderful company – and so impetuously, dangerously fluent with his pen. While he was Lord Berkeley's chaplain, one of his chores was to read to the Countess, Berkeley's wife, from Robert Boyle's *Meditations*. The solemn tone and far-fetched comparisons of the *Meditations* made it dull work, so

Swift composed his own *Meditations on a Broomstick*, inserted it into the book, and read his piece to the Countess. It was full of sage, ludicrous reflections, such as "But a broomstick, perhaps, you will say, is an emblem of a tree standing on its head; and pray what is man, but a topsy-turvy creature, his animal faculties perpetually mounted upon his rational, his head where his heels should be, grovelling on the earth!"

The Countess was deeply impressed; but when she praised the piece to friends and looked in the book for it, the deception was revealed. Luckily for Swift, she had a sense of humour.

POWERFUL ENEMIES

In public life Swift's inability to rein himself in often led to more serious consequences. He made implacable enemies among the grand and powerful – and none more so than the red-headed Coun-

tess of Somerset, a friend of Queen Anne, who understandably never forgave Swift for his poem *The Windsor Prophesy*, which made ruthless fun of 'carrots from Northumberland' and her marital disasters.

One way of avoiding the worst consequences of his jests was to publish anonymously or under a pseudonym. By this means Swift could hope to escape reprisals if he uttered dangerous thoughts – as he did in *The Drapier's Letters,* stirring up Irish opinion against William Wood's halfpence and English oppression in general. Sometimes Swift's anonymity had to be maintained life-long, as with his first masterpiece, *A Tale of a Tub,* which offended believers of all shades of religious opinion. Fortunately for his contemporary reputation, Swift's denials were widely disbelieved, and – despite temporary misattributions – the authorship of most of his works rapidly became known in his own lifetime.

However, Swift had an additional, purely literary reason for not putting his name to many of his works. He frequently wrote in the first person, assuming the character and employing the style of some other individual or type. Lemuel Gulliver, not Jonathan Swift, is the author of the *Travels*, and his nautical know-how and travel-book style did in fact send some of Swift's contemporaries to their atlases in an attempt to trace his journeys.

A Tale of a Tub is written by a hack author who shamelessly admits to padding the book with digressions to make some money, and whose superior 'modern' manner is made fun of by Swift. And *A Modest Proposal* is the work of a well-meaning but morally blind economist writing in the accepted jargon of the day ('a modest proposal' was itself a cliché, usually prefixed to the titles of pamphlets advocating new legislation). In other words, concealing his true identity enabled Swift to satirize men and manners with impunity, by means of parody.

AN ELABORATE HOAX

Not all of these personations were intended to deceive the reader for long; but Swift's more elaborate hoax, the *Bickerstaff Papers* (1708), did depend on preserving two assumed characters for a few weeks. To discredit a brazenly self-advertising almanac-writer and astrologer named John Partridge, Swift issued his own almanac under the signature 'Isaac Bickerstaff'. Casually planted among his other forecasts was a prediction that Partridge would die on 29 March.

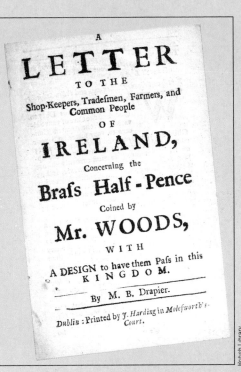

A LETTER TO THE Shop-Keepers, Tradesmen, Farmers, and Common People OF IRELAND, Concerning the Brass Half-Pence Coined by Mr. WOODS, WITH A DESIGN to have them Pass in this KINGDOM. By M. B. Drapier.

Dublin : Printed by J. Harding in Molesworth's Court.

British Library

Campaigner
In Ireland, Swift's propaganda (above) against coining halfpennies halted Government plans.

Whigs vs. Tories
The great preoccupation of the time was the debate between the recently formed Whig and Tory parties. It was carried on not only in the Lords and Commons (right) but in a barrage of political broadsheets (left). Swift sided squarely with the Tories, and was their prime pamphleteer – in effect, a peace-time propagandist. Neither he nor the genre was noted for gentleness or restraint, but he maintained that he toned down his views – 'I have often scratched out passages from papers and pamphlets . . . because I thought them too severe.'

Fotomas

As soon as that date had passed, Swift released a new pamphlet which, observant readers might have noted, appeared just in time for April Fool's Day. Now he wrote in the character of a gentleman who had decided to check up on Bickerstaff's prophesies – and declared that, to his surprise, Partridge had indeed passed away on 29 March. The hoax worked magnificently. The discomfited Partridge found it hard to convince people that he was still alive, and Swift and his friends were able to keep the joke going for some time, offering numerous proofs that, whatever Partridge might say, it stood to reason that he *must* be dead.

Swift's irony is often multi-layered, and although he was writing for a sophisticated society, he was often misunderstood. Did he mean it when he defended the maintenance of a purely nominal Christianity (not the real thing) with arguments based on its social usefulness? (If there were no officially estab-

Peter Tillemans : Parliament in 1710/Crown copyright. Reproduced with permission of the Controller of Her Majesty's Stationery Office

Sir Godfrey Kneller: Sir Richard Steele/National Portrait Gallery, London

Literary friend
One of Swift's close friends was Richard Steele (left), editor of The Tatler *(below) to which Swift contributed. After a political falling out, however, Steele used his new periodical,* The Guardian, *to make a vicious attack. 'Have I deserved this usage from Mr Steele?' cried an outraged Swift.*

British Library

Fotomas

lished religion for wits to rail against, they might set about the Government instead. And, after all, churches were extremely useful – for amours, business appointments and sleep.)

Given Swift's extremely non-dogmatic attitude towards religion, it was hard to be certain of his stance. Despite its elaborate structure and fictive authorship, *A Tale of a Tub* gave Swift a reputation as a dangerous sceptic that he found hard to live down, even after he attached an 'Author's Apology' to the 1710 edition. In the Apology he explained that "there generally runs an irony through the thread of the whole book, which the man of taste will observe and distinguish; and which will render such objections that have been made very weak and insignificant." However, in case such a broad hint should spoil the fun, Swift characteristically confused the issue by ending the Apology with a list of other works by the same author, including such contributions to scholarship as *A History of Ears* and *A Modest Defence of the Proceedings of the Rabble in All Ages*.

Although his mind teemed with words – he scribbled rhymes, riddles and doggerel when not more seriously engaged in literary work – Swift was a self-disciplined writer. However fanciful

his matter, he is always lucid, straightforward and forceful. He could also turn his pen to anything. Though best known as a prose satirist, he was also an accomplished poet in mock-serious vein. His political pamphlets are the product of a diamond-bright, if partisan, intelligence. And in private communications he revealed a different side of his personality, especially in the 'journal letters' to Esther Johnson and her companion, composed during his long stay in London. These were preserved by accident, and published posthumously as *Journal to Stella*.

The letters were written at the end of the day or first thing in the morning (often before Swift got out of bed), and intersperse the record of his political and social activities with errands run for 'the ladies' in Dublin and expressions of grumpy tenderness. They also include

Coffee house company
(above) Swift shared the contemporary taste for coffee houses – and for the lively debates that took place in them. He was also addicted to coffee – 'riches are nine parts in ten of all that is good in life, and health is the tenth; drinking coffee . . . is the eleventh.' In St James's coffee house he discussed politics and poetry, delivering himself of such opinions as 'your versifying . . . seems somewhat parallel to singing a psalm upon a ladder.'

passages written in a private 'little language' consisting of baby-talk and abbreviations in which Presto (Swift) wished MD [My dears] 'Nite deelest logues' [Goodnight, dearest rogues].

One irony seems never to have been appreciated by Swift. He published his literary works anonymously, and generally refused to take money for them, although he did demand and receive the large sum of £200 for *Gulliver*. He failed in his worldly ambitions, and was condemned to live ('like a poisoned rat in a hole') far from the centres of power and reputation. Yet the embittered exile enjoyed in full measure what so many other writers have craved: fame in his own time.

In fact Swift had several reputations – as the notorious author of *A Tale of a Tub*, as the one-man propaganda department of the 1710-14 Tory ministry, as a poet second only to his friend Alexander Pope, and as an Irish patriot steadfastly opposed to 'the tyranny and injustice of England in the treatment of this kingdom'.

Finally, with the publication of *Gulliver's Travels* in 1726, his fame spread far beyond the British Isles. His literary friend Dr John Arbuthnot predicted that the book would have 'as great a run as John Bunyan', and indeed it was immediately translated into French and read by the whole of fashionable Europe. Swift, always the ironist, only claimed for the *Travels*, 'They are admirable things, and will wonderfully mend the world.'

High and Low
The split between High and Low Church (left) greatly exercised the intellectuals of the time. A Tale of A Tub was Swift's contribution to the controversy.

'In everybody's hands'
The first printing of Gulliver's Travels sold out in a week. Swift's friends wrote to him in Ireland, declaring the book 'the admiration of all men'. It was soon available in translation (right) throughout Europe.

Fotomas

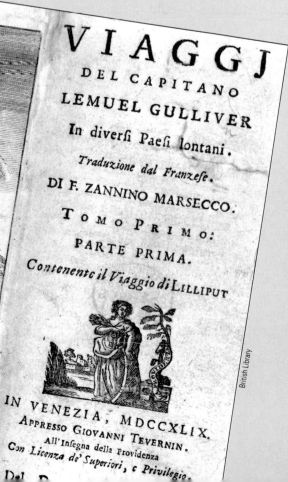

VIAGGJ
DEL CAPITANO
LEMUEL GULLIVER
In diverfi Paefi lontani.
Traduzione dal Franzefe.
DI F. ZANNINO MARSECCO.
Tomo Primo:
PARTE PRIMA.
Contenente il Viaggio di LILLIPUT

IN VENEZIA, MDCCXLIX.
APPRESSO GIOVANNI TEVERNIN.
All'Infegna della Providenza
Con *Licenza de' Superiori, e Privilegio.*

British Library

Torn between concern and contempt for humanity, Jonathan Swift found his ideal mode of expression in acerbic satire. *The Battle of the Books*, written in 1697-98 and published in 1704, is a relatively light-hearted fantasy. It appeared with *A Tale of a Tub*, a controversial widely read allegorical tale about the various rival brands of Christianity.

Swift's years of influence in London produced a masterpiece never intended for publication – the letters to Esther Johnson, now known as *Journal to Stella*. From the same period, his pamphlet *The Conduct of the Allies* (1711) identified Swift with the Tory cause; its collapse propelled him into Irish 'exile', where he wrote vigorously in defence of his fellow-countrymen's interests. His personal and public disappointments are reflected in the pessimistic strain of *Gulliver's Travels* (1726). Despairing of both Irish and English, Swift wrote the most savage of all his works, *A Modest Proposal* (1729), in which he voices a drastic, hideous solution.

THE BATTLE OF THE BOOKS

◆ 1704 ◆

The books of St James's Library in London engage in desperate combat (below) in this mock epic prompted by a scholarly debate about the respective merits of ancient and modern writers. Swift's patron, Sir William Temple, was on the side of the 'Ancients', and Swift's sympathies also lie with them. In the story, an edition of Homer's poetry leads the Ancients' cavalry, while philosophers Plato and Aristotle command their bowmen. Ranged on the other side are moderns such as Milton, Descartes and Dryden (Swift's cousin).

Mary Evans Picture Library/Hand colouring Ann Hemming

A TALE OF A TUB

◆ 1704 ◆

Three sons (above) represent the three strands of western Christianity in this complicated, allegorical story. Peter (the Roman Catholic Church), Martin (the Church of England) and Jack (the Nonconformist sects) are each left a coat in their father's will, on condition that they do not add or subtract so much as a thread. But worldly influences are too much for them – especially Peter, who falsifies the will and decks out his coat with satin, silk and embroidery. His brothers are misled until they discover the true contents of the will and throw off Peter's (the Pope's) authority, whereupon he goes mad. But whereas Jack becomes obsessed with undoing Peter's work, even though this involves damaging the coat, Martin – representing the Anglican 'middle way' – takes the only sensible sartorial course . . . The book is interspersed with 'digressions', one of which – *Digression on Madness* – implies that the author is in fact a lunatic himself.

Fotomas

JOURNAL TO STELLA
◆ 1766-8 ◆

Addressed to Esther Johnson (below) and her companion Rebecca Dingley, these 65 rambling, gossipy, grumbling letters were written between September 1710 and June 1713, the period Swift spent in London enjoying his greatest political influence. They give a vivid picture of Swift in his lodgings at St James's; with his drunken servant Patrick; as the intimate of ministers, busy writing in their cause; going out into society and playing picquet and 'whisk' (whist); and cultivating friendships with fellow writers such as Addison and Pope.

National Gallery of Ireland

Fotomas

A MODEST PROPOSAL
◆ 1729 ◆

One-year-olds make 'excellent nutritive meat' (above). On this repulsive assertion is based Swift's bitterly ironic proposal "for preventing the children of the poor people of Ireland from being a burden to their parents and country". The idea – to sell 100,000 meaty babies each year to "persons of quality and fortune" – is logically argued. There will be fewer Catholics (the "principal breeders"); the poor will at last own something of real value and men will treat their pregnant wives as well as they treat mares in foal . . .

THE CONDUCT OF THE ALLIES
◆ 1711 ◆

"Ten glorious campaigns are passed [right] and now at last, like the sick man, we are just expiring with all sorts of good symptoms." So runs Swift's most famous political pamphlet in defence of the Tory policy of ending the long, unsuccessful war against France (the War of the Spanish Succession), waged by England in alliance with Holland and Austria since 1702. He argued that Blenheim and the other great victories won by the Duke of Marlborough had failed to end the war and were ruining England. Since England's allies had let her down, there was no moral obligation for her to fight on in order to put an Austrian Hapsburg on the Spanish throne. In a devastating personal attack, Swift declared that the war had been deliberately prolonged, against the national interests, for one reason only – to enrich Marlborough. Swift's pamphlet had an immediate impact, greatly strengthening anti-war feelings.

The Art of War/Victoria and Albert Museum

Ravaged Ireland

A Protestant Britain, nervous and unforgiving of those who had fought for a Catholic king, constructed a social and economic cage in which to imprison the Irish, and put English keepers in charge.

In July 1690 two royal armies faced each other across an Irish river to fight for the British Crown. This was the Battle of the Boyne, and the armies belonged to the Protestant William of Orange and the Catholic James II. Eighteen months previously, James had lost the English throne to William and Mary (his daughter), and now, with the backing of France, he sought to regain it from the intermediate ground of Ireland. James was heavily defeated, however, and fled to France, but his army fought on, hoping to win favourable peace terms.

A year later the surrender of Limerick City marked the end of their struggle. William's initial willingness to deal fairly with the vanquished was drowned out by the fears of his Protestant English and Anglo-Irish subjects. The support given to James II by the Catholic Irish had terrified them and they were determined to guarantee their future safety by having absolute 'Protestant Ascendancy' in Ireland.

A great many Irishmen followed James II into exile in France. These soldier-refugees were known as the 'Wild Geese' and in Swift's lifetime 150,000 of them died in the service of France alone. As the Wild Geese left, many Protestants returned to Ireland from England, where, like the young Swift, they had found sanctuary during the war. Although these Anglo-Irish Protestants had their differences with Ulster Presbyterians, they were united in their loyalty to the English Crown. Despite victory, however, they could not feel secure as a minority in overwhelmingly Catholic Ireland, fearing that the Wild Geese, with foreign aid, might return to oust them.

THE PENAL LAWS

The Irish Parliament did little more than rubber stamp measures passed in England. Even given the political bias of its members, it could pass no law without the consent of the King and the English Privy Council. Catholics were barred from it by a qualifying oath which involved a detailed denial of their faith. In fact all important Government and Church positions were held by men appointed in England – and many of them took their salaries without even living in Ireland.

Posted to Ireland against his will, Swift did not like being 'neglected' in Dublin when he could have been 'with the best company in London'. But he was too principled to be indifferent to the problems of the community he found himself in; and unlike other members of the Protestant Ascendancy he was not afraid of being branded a Jacobite (supporter of King James) for speaking out against the consequences of English oppression.

Battle of the Boyne
(above) Popular opinion drove James II from the English throne, but not from the hearts of the Catholic Irish. He saw Ireland as the perfect base for making a renewed bid for power. The struggle conducted on Irish soil was not, therefore, to determine who ruled Ireland, but who ruled England. It was known as The War of the Two Kings, and was won by William III at the Battle of the Boyne (1690) and the Battle of Aughrim (1691). Both battles are still commemorated by Protestant 'Orangemen'.

de Wyck: Battle of the Boyne/National Gallery of Ireland

William III
When William of Orange (left) invaded Ireland and defeated the supporters of James II (right) the tide of influence turned in favour of the English monarchy. An Anglo-Irish infrastructure consolidated and protected the Protestant victory, severely curbing the rights, hopes and freedom of the Catholic majority in Ireland.

Unknown: William III/National Portrait Gallery, London

Sir Godfrey Kneller: James II/National Portrait Gallery, London

country, on pain of the penalty for High Treason – hanging and quartering. Ordinary priests had to register with the government if they wished to celebrate Mass, and unregistered priests faced transportation if they were caught, hanging if they returned. At one stage castration was proposed as the penalty for first-offending unregistered priests.

The Protestant Ascendancy would never be secure while Catholics owned property. According to the Penal Laws a Catholic could not even own a horse worth more than five pounds. If a Protestant saw a horse he liked, he could give its Catholic owner five pounds and take it. No Catholic could inherit land that had once belonged to a Protestant. Catholics could inherit from other Catholics, but they were forbidden to buy land, lend money against mortgages, or take a lease lasting longer than 31 years. When a Catholic landowner died, his eldest son was given one year in which to become a Protestant. If he did, he became the owner of the entire estate. If he did not, the estate was split into equal portions between all the sons. These laws were extremely effective, for by 1703 only 14 per cent of Irish land was in Catholic-Irish hands; by 1778 scarcely five per cent.

'MERE IRISH'

The Penal Laws resulted in a sort of apartheid based on religion. Many of the Catholics with the most to lose – big landowners and lawyers – converted to Anglicanism. But, of course, apart from the restrictions which drove their religion underground and the obligation to pay tithes to an alien church, the 'mere Irish' (as the poor Catholic majority was known) were hardly affected by the Penal Laws relating to property and education.

Survival rather than further rebellion preoccupied the common people. The natural leaders had left with the Wild Geese, and their new masters (some had acquired forfeited Catholic estates or been rewarded with land as spoils of war) were interested only in rent. Many of the landlords preferred to live in England, and in 1725 Swift

Puppet Parliament
The Irish Parliament (left) had been obliged, since 1494, to submit its legislation for ratification by the English Parliament. After 1720, Westminster could legislate for Ireland.

Property and power
Phoenix Lodge (below) housed the Lord Lieutenant of Ireland. All the great estates were owned by English or Anglo-Irish.

He had contempt for 'the club', the members of the Irish Parliament who did nothing to prevent the ruin of the country they claimed to represent.

Not surprisingly, there was no opposition in this 'club' to the series of Acts, known as the Penal Laws, passed in the 35 years after the Battle of the Boyne. The Penal Laws were designed to suppress Catholicism and obliterate what remained of native Irish culture and were unique as a form of religious oppression in that they were directed against the majority of the population.

Catholics were now effectively excluded from the legal profession, all government offices and commissions in the army and navy. Catholic tradesmen could not join guilds and they could not take on more than two apprentices. It was an offence for Catholics to run schools in Ireland or to send their children to be educated abroad (which is what surviving families began to do). Senior Catholic clergy were banished from the

estimated that absentees drew one-third of the revenue yielded by Irish land. Rents spiralled as these absentees allowed 'middlemen' to manage their estates. The middlemen let small tracts of land on very short terms, auctioning them off to the highest bidder when the lease expired. As a churchman and a member of the Ascendancy, Swift did not object to the Penal Laws. But he could not condone needless, counter-productive, hypocritical injustice.

The countryside was always on the brink of economic crisis, and it was in Swift's time that famine and emigration became commonplace. In the famines of 1726 and 1729 thousands died; in the great famine of 1739–41 a fifth of the population, 400,000 people, starved to death. Visitors frequently compared Irish peasants to Russian serfs, and Swift wrote that any stranger 'would be apt to think himself travelling in Lapland or Iceland, rather than in a country so favoured by nature as ours . . . The miserable dress, and diet, and dwelling of the people; the general desolation in most parts of the kingdom; the old seats of the nobility and gentry all in ruins and no new ones in their stead; the families of farmers who pay great rents living in filth and nastiness upon buttermilk and potatoes, without a shoe or stocking to their feet, or a house so convenient as an English hogsty to receive them.' He declared that animals in England had a higher standard of living.

Early 18th-century Dublin was notorious for its population of beggars and muggers, and Swift, Dean of the city's cathedral, blamed the appalling state of the countryside for this problem. It was after the famine of 1729 that he suggested his most barbed, bitterly ironic solution. This was *A Modest*

Reduced to beggary
A crippling economic policy caused havoc with the poor of Ireland. Famine was recurrent, beggars a common sight (below).

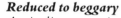

An industry destroyed
The thriving Irish wool trade (above), a pillar of Ireland's economy, was stifled by the 1699 Woollen Act. This ensured a monopoly for England, and effectively placed all that Ireland produced at her disposal.

Proposal for Preventing the Children of Poor People in Ireland from Being a Burden to their Parents or the Country, and for making them Beneficial to the Public. Since the landlords were effectively devouring the parents, why not make a new meat trade out of poor children, said Swift: 'a young healthy child, well nursed, is at a year old a most delicious, nourishing and wholesome food, whether stewed, roasted, baked or boiled, and I make no doubt that it will equally serve well in a fricassee or a ragout.'

THE EXPLOITED EMPIRE
Swift had no particular affection for the ordinary people and little understanding of their culture. In *A Modest Proposal* he was criticizing the shiftlessness of the babies' parents as much as the irresponsibility of their social betters. What made him a patriot, almost in spite of himself, was his outrage at the fact that, unlike their Scottish counterparts, all Irish people were treated by the English government as second-class subjects.

He observed how the kingdom of Ireland, once England's sister isle, was fast becoming an empire to be exploited rather than developed by the mother country. Swift referred to Ireland as a lady seduced by a fine gentleman (England), who had now abandoned her in order to marry another lady

James Malton: Custom House, Dublin/National Gallery of Ireland

James Malton: Marine School, Dublin/National Gallery of Ireland

Nothing to declare
New customs duties levied on Irish goods (the Customs House, Dublin, is pictured left) creamed off the income from exported cattle. The Navigation Acts, which channelled Irish goods through English ports and gave English shipping a monopoly in the carriage of Irish cargoes (below left), were an iniquitous constraint on Irish trade. Swift summed up Ireland's trade as 'nothing worth mentioning except the linen of the north, a trade casual, corrupted, and at mercy, and some butter from Cork.' Ireland's merchants had all 'dwindled to pedlars and cheats'.

Wood's Halfpence
(below) In fighting the decision to grant one man the right to coin Irish money, Swift enunciated the fundamental principle at issue: 'All government without the consent of the governed is the very essence of slavery.' His Drapier's Letters stirred Protestants and Catholics to nationalistic indignation – 'the rage was universal'. Wood's patent was withdrawn.

(Scotland). It was particularly unfortunate for Ireland that her potentially prosperous economy could rival England's: it therefore paid both to milk and to weaken her economically.

The Navigation Acts, by which Irish trade could be conducted only through English ports and in English ships, had disastrous effects. According to Swift this meant that Ireland's harbours were about as useful as a beautiful view to a man in prison. The greatest single blow to the Irish economy was the Woollen Act of 1699, which destroyed the wool industry by prohibiting the export of Irish manufactured wool to anywhere but England. The raw wool could be exported only to specified English ports, which gave England a monopoly.

Crippling duties were also payable on Irish cattle imported by England. But instead of reacting to these adverse market forces by turning their land over to arable farming, the landowners persisted in using it for grazing. This was, in Swift's words, an absurdity 'that a wild Indian would be ashamed of'; but the reason was obvious. A grazier's cabin was much cheaper to provide than decent farmhouses: 'Thus a vast tract of land, where twenty or thirty farmers lived, together with their cottagers and labourers in their several cabins, became all desolate and easily managed by one or two herdsmen and their boys.'

Although an illegal wool trade carried on – smuggled Irish wool being bartered for claret, brandy and silk from France – the weavers starved or emigrated as a result of the Woollen Act. St Patrick's Cathedral was right at the heart of Dublin's wool-working district, so the Dean was personally aware of the weavers' plight. He was known for his charitable efforts on their behalf, and they returned his interest with affectionate celebrations for his birthday every year. It was no accident that Swift adopted the identity of 'M. B., draper of Francis Street' when, in 1724, he led the campaign against 'William Wood's Halfpence'.

'FILTHY TRASH'

William Wood was an English manufacturer who obtained a patent from the Crown to mint copper money for Ireland. It was actually the king's mistress who acquired the patent, and she sold it to Wood for £10,000. Like so much other Irish business, this contract had been handed to Wood without regard for Ireland's currency needs and without adequate supervision of his get-rich-quick methods. Many feared that the massive increase in copper coins would drive all gold and silver money from the kingdom, and that Wood would also debase his coins to increase his profit.

Swift weighed into this controversy in the person of a no-nonsense draper who denounced the Wood deal in a series of scathing pamphlets, *The Drapier's Letters*. Through them Swift became the spokesman for the resistance to Wood, and his vivid arguments found a ready audience, especially in Dublin. 'One and All', he urged the people, 'refuse this *Filthy Trash*'. William Wood was yet another 'Blood-sucker' and a boycott of his coins was the best strategy against him.

The Lord Lieutenant offered a reward of £300 for the real identity of the author of *The Drapier's Letters*. But the Dean, alias the draper, was so popular, his arguments so well-supported, that he

Irish Volunteers
The American Revolution obliged England to withdraw troops from Ireland, needing all its manpower and resources for the struggle overseas. In their place, brigades of Protestant Irish 'Volunteers' (left) were formed to keep the peace. Most of the senior officers were also members of the Irish Parliament, and it no longer seemed expedient to deny the country independent legislation. Westminster therefore bought loyalty by renouncing its right to pass laws for Ireland. The English grip was loosening.

was not betrayed. The authorities could not even persuade a Protestant Grand Jury to agree to the prosecution of the printer involved. In the face of the campaign, Wood's project was abandoned in 1725 and from that time the English government never again granted an individual the right to coin Irish money.

THE ACT OF UNION

Swift continually recommended boycotts of English products – the slogan 'burn everything English but their coal' was adapted from one of his phrases. (In fact the word 'boycott' did not enter the language until more than a century after Swift's death, when, in 1880, an English land agent of that name was ostracized by his Irish tenants). But in Swift's day the 'second-class subjects' were too demoralized to follow his advice, and their masters remembered the recent war too well to develop an independent attitude to Westminster. When Swift died in 1745, Ireland was peaceful but still miserable.

The next generation of the Protestant Ascendancy was more secure and more liberal – their new country houses did not need to be fortified. Influenced by the revolt of the American colonists, they became more patriotically Irish. Henry Grattan led the movement for an independent parliament for Ireland, which was granted in 1782. In his victory speech he said 'Spirit of Swift, spirit of Molyneaux, your genius has prevailed. Ireland is now a nation.' Many of the Penal Laws had been relaxed or fallen into disuse, and in the same year the Catholic clergy was legalized.

Seven years later the French Revolution inspired the first Irish republican movement, led by Wolfe Tone. The United Irishmen hoped that the Scots-Irish Presbyterians of the north would rise with the Catholic peasants of the south and, with French

An enlightened view
Henry Grattan, leader of the Irish 'Patriot' Party, addressed Parliament in 1782 with his 'Declaration of Irish Rights' (below), the result of legislative independence. He also maintained that Catholics must not be left without a voice. He failed to win their emancipation, however, overwhelmed by the indifference of fellow MPs.

aid, overthrow the government to set up an Irish republic. But their organization was riddled with spies, the French did not help and the resulting uprising of 1798 was brutally put down.

After this bloody nightmare the badly shaken Ascendancy meekly submitted to the British Government's abolition of their independent parliament. In exchange they would have complete union with England and Irish representation at Westminster. In 1801 the Act of Union was passed. Doubtless Swift would have approved: this Union was the injured lady's wedding to the suitor who had wronged her in the past. But for the Catholic working people it was a forced marriage which would result in a lastingly unquiet nuptial bed.

LEWIS CARROLL

◆ *1832-1898* ◆

The Reverend Charles Lutwidge Dodgson, alias Lewis Carroll, was an extraordinary man who led three lives. One was as a shy, unsociable mathematics don (fellow and tutor) at Christ Church College, Oxford. The second was as a renowned child photographer. And that for which he is best remembered is as the author of the brilliantly inventive *Alice* stories, inspired by and written for two little girls named Alice. Only at home in the company of children such as these, he died a 'lonely bachelor' at 65.

Childhood's Captive

University undergraduates found him humourless and dry, a scholar living in an ivory tower. But with children the Oxford don turned into a spinner of tales, and a friend on the journey through childhood.

On 4 July 1862, a 30-year-old Oxford don, the Reverend Charles Dodgson, accompanied by his clerical friend Robinson Duckworth, took out a boat and rowed the three daughters of the Dean of Christ Church to Godstow, taking tea on the river bank before returning. Not an unusual event in itself, but one which was to become part of the mythology of English literature. For it was during this journey that the shy, thin, Victorian don first told a story that so interested one of the little girls, Alice Liddell, that she begged Dodgson to write it down for her.

Thus Dodgson created one of the best loved and most influential of children's books, *Alice's Adventures in Wonderland*. Like Dodgson himself, Alice is 'loving and gentle...ready to accept the wildest impossibilities with all that utter trust that only dreamers know...and with eager enjoyment of Life that comes only in the happy hours of childhood.'

Charles Lutwidge Dodgson was born on 27 January 1832 at Daresbury Parsonage in Cheshire where his father, Charles Dodgson senior, was rector. Charles was the eldest in a family of eleven children: four boys and seven girls. As a boy and a young man he was unusually attached to his mother whose kindness and sympathy he was to treasure always. His father, though strict, was by no means tyrannical and the boy grew up in a well-ordered, stable and comfortable environment.

IDYLLIC CHILDHOOD

In 1843, the family moved to Croft on the Yorkshire/Durham border. Here, in a vast house equipped with bake-house, brewery and laundry, managed by plentiful servants, Dodgson spent what he was later to regard as an idyllic childhood. With the rectory went enough livestock to provide all the dairy produce, eggs and bacon that the Dodgsons needed. The family lived an almost entirely self-contained, tribal existence, making few contacts with the world outside the vicarage gardens. But like other boys of his class Dodgson was sent away to school. At Richmond, where he boarded despite the fact that it was only ten miles from home, he soon showed his academic brilliance. He possessed 'a very uncommon share of genius' reported his headmaster at the end of his first term.

From Richmond, Dodgson went on to Rugby. Four years after the death of its illustrious headmaster Dr Thomas Arnold, the worst excesses of bullying and brutality had been stamped out. But the life of the school came as a shock to the sensitive, sheltered Dodgson. He had a severe stammer, which, together with his studiousness and poor performance at games, marked him out for the classroom tyrants. Nothing, he was to admit years later, would have ever induced

Key Dates

1832 born at Daresbury, Cheshire

1846-9 at Rugby School

1851 enters Christ Church, Oxford. Mother dies

1855 teaches Maths at Oxford; takes up photography

1861 ordained deacon

1862 boat trip in which the *Alice* story unfolds

1865 *Alice's Adventures in Wonderland* published

1868 father dies

1871 *Through the Looking-Glass* published

1898 dies at Guildford, Surrey

All Saints Church
Memorial windows based on Tenniel's illustrations for Alice honour Daresbury's illustrious father and son. Charles Dodgson senior was vicar here from 1827-43, and it was at the nearby parsonage that the future Lewis Carroll was born.

Archdeacon Dodgson
Charles Dodgson's father was a classical scholar, author of several books on religion and, like his son, was fascinated by mathematics. He also had a similar sense of fun. Years later his son wrote 'The greatest blow that has ever fallen on my life was the death, nearly thirty years ago, of my own dear father.'

Derek Forss

National Portrait Gallery, London

Rugby School
(right) The young Charles Dodgson excelled in his academic work while at Rugby, but was less than enthusiastic about his time there: 'I cannot say that I look back upon my life at Public [private] School with any sensations of pleasure or that any earthly considerations would induce me to go through my three years again.' On leaving, he returned home to Croft.

Croft Rectory
The Dodgsons moved to the spacious rectory at Croft in 1843. Situated on the Yorkshire/Durham border, it had more than enough space for a family of 12 – with four reception rooms, a nursery, a butler's pantry and a housekeeper's room.

him to repeat the three years spent at Rugby. With time he learned to cope with the traumas by day, but he was never to forget what he called the 'annoyance at night' to which he was subjected.

Growing up did not come easily. At the age of 18, on the threshold of manhood, he postponed his expulsion from adolescence – "where Childhood's dreams are twined/In Memory's mystic band" – by returning home to Croft to spend one last year at home before going up to Oxford.

On 24 January 1851 he entered his father's old college of Christ Church. Two days later his dream of childhood ended tragically with the sudden and premature death of his adored mother. He felt the loss keenly and the memory stayed with him throughout his life. Nineteen years after the event he was to write to his sister Mary on the birth of her first son: 'May you be to him what your own dear mother was to *her* eldest son. I can hardly utter for your son a better wish than that.' That tiny boy, christened Stuart Collingwood, was to be Dodgson's biographer 47 years later.

Hard-working, serious-minded, fastidious and devout, Dodgson seemed to embody all the solid virtues of mid-Victorian England, with none of its vices. He committed none of the follies normally associated with youth. He did not get drunk or pursue the less respectable forms of female society available to young men of means at the time. He did not fall in love or even show the least interest in girls of his own age.

UNDERGRADUATE DAYS

As an undergraduate, the pattern of Dodgson's life became set. Remaining aloof from his contemporaries, he nevertheless delighted in the company of children. Only with children did he lose his acute nervousness and stammer, and was light-hearted, witty and imaginative. Dr Thomas Fowler, who accompanied Dodgson on a 'reading party' to Whitby during the Long Vacation of 1854, recalled how Dodgson 'used to sit on a rock on the beach, telling stories to a circle of eager young listeners of both sexes'. He became adept at befriending children, and carried a black bag full of games and puzzles with which to attract their interest.

But even at Whitby, work was a priority. As he wrote to his sister Mary, he was getting on 'very swimmingly' with Integral Calculus. The long years of sustained study were duly rewarded that October with a first class degree in Mathematics. The quiet, 22-year-old Dodgson was now almost fully fledged as an Oxford don.

'I don't think he ever laughed', recalled a former child friend, Ellen Rowell, many years later, 'though his own particular crooked smile, so whimsical, so

tender, so ironic, was in and out all the time.' But to the undergraduates he was now obliged to teach he was the quintessential don with a 'singularly unsmiling and perfunctory manner'. Essentially a self-centred man, he lacked all interest in his students and seemed almost oblivious of the college servants who were at his beck and call for almost half a century.

Only during the Long Vacation did he permit himself any relaxation, although long, rigorous walks were a feature of term-time. After savouring the delights of the Isle of Wight for several summers, he settled for the charm of Eastbourne, returning to the same lodgings every year for twenty consecutive summers. A creature of the very strictest habits, Dodgson neither sought nor enjoyed change. Only once did he venture abroad – rather unusually to Russia.

Dodgson the dull Oxford don is, however, only a partial portrait. By his dedication to two separate art forms – literature and photography – he transcended the confines of the university.

It was his uncle Skeffington Lutwidge who first introduced Dodgson to photography. From May 1856 to July 1880, capturing beautiful images became virtually an obsession for him. He pursued it single-mindedly, becoming one of the foremost portrait photographers of his day and, arguably, the best photographer of children in the 19th century.

DISCOVERING PHOTOGRAPHY

In the studio he built for himself above his rooms in Christ Church, Dodgson was a man transformed. He lost his shyness and reserve, becoming almost tyrannical in his pursuit of perfection. Photography was then in its infancy, dominated by the formal portrait, and here, as in his writing, Dodgson challenged the conventions of the time. He encouraged naturalism, placing his subjects in a natural setting and attempting realistic, casual poses. Ruskin, Tennyson, Millais and the actress Ellen Terry (who became a lifelong friend) all sat for him, as did hundreds of children.

Dodgson's first meeting with four-year-old Alice Liddell was when he was invited by the Dean, her father, to photograph her and her two sisters in the gardens of the Deanery one day in April 1856. The photographic session was not a success – 'they were not patient sitters' he noted in his diary – but Dodgson was captivated by Alice. The feeling was to last almost ten years, until soon after the success of *Alice in Wonderland*.

Family portrait
(above left) Dodgson made this photographic study of his sisters and brother Edwin when he was 25.

Ellen Terry
In 1856 Dodgson saw a production of A Winter's Tale *in which a nine-year-old girl made her acting debut. The girl was Ellen Terry, and Dodgson was instantly enraptured. In his mind she became 'the one I have always most wished to meet', but that fateful moment was not to happen for another eight years. However, when they did eventually meet they became fast friends, and two years later he set to work on his first play,* Morning Clouds, *specifically for the great actress.*

Opening of the Great Exhibition by David Roberts. Reproduced by Gracious Permission of Her Majesty the Queen

THE MAD HATTER

It seems that *Alice's* illustrator, Tenniel, following Carroll's wishes, drew his Mad Hatter to resemble a certain Theophilus Carter, a well-known furniture dealer who lived near Oxford. Not only did Carter always wear a top hat, but he was renowned in the area for his eccentric ideas and inventions. In the Great Exhibition of 1851, Carter displayed his 'alarm clock bed', a contraption which woke the sleeper by literally tossing him out of bed at a pre-determined time.

Carroll would certainly have seen the bed at Crystal Palace and would have been familiar with the unusual figure of Carter around the streets of Oxford. The prevalence of furniture in the Tea-Party episode – the table, the writing-desk, the armchair, and the fascination with time, also point to a strong Theophilus Carter connection.

The Great Exhibition
(above) The year 1851 marked the opening of the Great Exhibition in the Crystal Palace. Arranged and organized by Prince Albert, it formed a landmark in Victorian history and drew visitors from all over the world. Dodgson was spellbound by it – there were mechanical birds, an amazing crystal fountain, and colossal, lifelike statues. To the master of dream-worlds it looked 'like a sort of fairyland.'

Few of Dodgson's infatuations with little girls outlasted their puberty. Ellen Terry, aware of this tendency, declared after their friendship had weathered this 'difficult' time, that 'he was as fond of me as he could be of anyone over the age of ten.' 'About nine out of ten...of my child-friendships got shipwrecked at the critical point "where the stream and the river meet"', Dodgson himself admitted years later, 'and the child-friends, once so affectionate, became uninteresting acquaintants, whom I have no wish to see again.'

Today there is a tendency to think that Dodgson's delight in dressing little girls in boys' clothes and in photographing them nude, or as he put it more coyly 'sans habillement', indicates some form of sexual deviancy. But there is little to suggest that his interest was primarily or even partially sexual. In the vast library of letters he wrote throughout his life (98,721 by his own calculations), there is no suggestion of anything in the least improper. They testify to a man unusually anxious to avoid the slightest whiff of scandal. When writing to his friend Miss E. Gertrude Thompson, inviting her to Oxford, he was most anxious that she came only with her parents' consent. This is perhaps not surprising in an age when almost all contact between unmarried men and women could only occur in public, but excessively prudish in the case of Miss Thompson who was then in her 30s.

Likewise there is no hint of a sexual interest in little girls in the nine surviving volumes of his diary. Only in *Pillow Problems*, which, despite its suggestive title, is concerned with 72 problems of algebra, plane geometry and trigonometry, does he mention 'unholy thoughts, which torture with their hateful presence the fancy that would fain be pure'. But this is scant evidence of a man unduly tormented by the rule of celibacy to which he was bound as an ordained deacon.

However, Dodgson was only too aware that his interest in nude photography had set tongues wagging. Perhaps it was for this reason that, in a typically cut-and-dried manner, he decided in July 1880 to give up photography for ever.

EARLY WRITINGS

But it was, of course, as a writer that Dodgson, under the pen-name Lewis Carroll, was to achieve fame. His beginning as a writer had not been entirely auspicious. As a child he had shown an unusual interest in words and in his teens had written, illustrated and produced what he called his 'domestic journalism'. This consisted in a series of little magazines with titles such as *The Comet, Will-o'-the-Wisp* and *The Rectory Umbrella*. In these Dodgson first developed his talent for nonsense verse and humorous short stories.

While staying at Whitby in 1854 Dodgson had had a poem and story published in the local *Gazette*. His work was also published in the *Oxonian Advertiser*, though consistently turned down by *Punch*. But it was the editor Edmund Yates who encouraged Dodgson's writing and prompted him to adopt a *nom de plume*. From a list of four supplied by Dodgson, Yates chose Lewis Carroll, derived, Dodgson said, by reversing his first two names and latinizing them, 'Ludwidge...Ludovic...Louis...and Charles...'.

Yates was also the first to publish a version of 'Jabberwocky' in 1856, although it was, of course, with *Alice* that Lewis Carroll became famous. It was, after a sluggish start, a phenomenal success, assuring Dodgson of a comfortable income for the rest of his life. But it had been created under trying circumstances. Rarely can a publisher have had a more exacting author than Dodgson. His demand to be involved and check every detail of the production process even went as far as his supplying a diagram showing how the parcels containing copies of the book should be properly packaged and tied.

LITERARY SUCCESS

Alice in Wonderland and *Through the Looking-Glass* were immensely popular. Together, 180,000 copies were sold during Dodgson's lifetime, although literary success and fame did little to change the pattern of Dodgson's life. In term-time he wrote mathematical texts, then spent the holidays in Eastbourne. After the death of his father in 1868 he bought a house called 'The Chestnuts' in Guildford for his unmarried sisters, and spent Christmas there each year. With the extra income provided by his books he was able to resign from his lectureship – always a heavy responsibility – and take on the job of Curator at Christ Church. This

Photo by Lewis Carroll/Mansell Collection

A KINDRED SPIRIT

Born in 1824 in rural Aberdeenshire, the author George MacDonald was a friend of both Alfred, Lord Tennyson and Lewis Carroll. He wrote more than 20 novels in his lifetime but is remembered almost exclusively for his children's fiction, notably *At the Back of the North Wind*.

Unlike other children's fiction at the time, MacDonald's writings was dreamlike and fantastical, comparable possibly to Tolkien who was to write his famous *The Lord of the Rings* trilogy some 80 years later. In Carroll's day, books for children were almost exclusively moralistic; they taught religious ideals and notions of good and evil. Sober, humourless poems formed the staple diet of Victorian children's reading and often had to be learned by heart and recited in front of their 'elders and betters'. The kind of writing MacDonald and Carroll engaged in was revolutionary – it allowed, even encouraged, children to be and think like children.

Carroll took photographs of the MacDonald children, and they inspected the *Alice* manuscript before it was submitted to the publishers. Six-year-old Greville loved it, and declared 60,000 copies of it should be printed!

MacDonald and the North Wind
On the left is a contemporary cartoon of George MacDonald and above is one of the fantasy illustrations from his best-loved children's book, At the Back of the North Wind.

Mary Evans Picture Library

Alice and her sister
On 26 April 1856, Charles Dodgson encountered the four-year-old Alice Liddell (shown seated in the chair) for the first time. He could not have imagined the extent to which she was to transform his life.

Riverside college
(right) This watercolour by J. M. W. Turner shows Dodgson's college, Christ Church, where he spent much of his life as student, lecturer and curator.

Artistic circles
(below) Dodgson mixed with both academics and artists, such as Julia Margaret Cameron, who took this photograph of G.F. Watts.

Ashmolean Museum, Oxford

BBC Hulton Picture Library

entailed supplying the College with its groceries, wine and fuel, managing the servants and balancing the budget. As always, he performed his duties with extreme care and punctiliousness.

Fame as an author widened his circle of friends and acquaintances. Lord Salisbury, a future Prime Minister, was one. Invited to Hatfield House, Dodgson entertained the children as ever with stories and games and puzzles. At these and other occasions Carroll showed his instinctive rapport with children: 'Carroll was expected at a children's party, and he arrived crawling on hands and knees, covered with a bear rug, and growling. It was the wrong address – a tremendous shock for the parlourmaid who opened the door.'

But despite the adulation of children and adults alike, he felt himself to be a 'lonely bachelor'. As the years passed he became increasingly concerned with his health, taking up the study of medicine in his usual methodical manner. Though perhaps lonely at times, he was not one given to bemoan his fate. In a letter dated August 1894 he wrote, 'my life is so strangely free from all trial and trouble that I cannot doubt my own happiness is one of the talents entrusted to me . . .'

'DEATH IS OVER'

There were still child-friends, and he even kept up with one former child-friend, Gertrude Chataway, to whom he had dedicated *The Hunting of the Snark*. Now in his sixties, Dodgson suffered increasingly from a condition known as synovitis which affected his knees and prevented him from walking. Sometimes he was bed-ridden for months. In the end, however, it was an attack of bronchitis that proved fatal. On 14 January 1898 Charles Dodgson died at about 2.30 in the afternoon in his sisters' house in Guildford. Some years before he had confided in a letter 'I sometimes think what a grand thing it will be to be able to say to oneself, "Death is *over* now; there is not *that* experience to be faced again."'

ALICE IN WONDERLAND
and Through the Looking-Glass

The best, but by no means the only way to enjoy the *Alice* books is to follow the King of Hearts' advice: "Begin at the beginning, and go on till you come to the end: then stop."

A Mad Tea Party by Arthur Rackham. With permission of Barbara Edwards, daughter of the artist

*A*lice's Adventures in Wonderland and *Through the Looking-Glass* are among the most charming and celebrated of all children's books, and their appeal remains undiminished to a vast adult readership. Together they form one of the most quoted works in the English language. At the time of publication they were considered extraordinary for their unsentimental and wry attitude to children. Children of the upper middle classes were then 'seen but not heard' and their fiction was shrouded in misty romanticism. Lewis Carroll broke the mould with *Alice*.

ALICE IN WONDERLAND

Alice is sitting with her sister on a bank, bored and sleepy. Suddenly a white rabbit runs by in

> *"Dear, dear! How queer everything is today! And yesterday things went on just as usual. I wonder if I've been changed in the night? Let me think: was I the same when I got up this morning? I almost think I can remember feeling a little different."*

a state of great excitement. Alice follows the rabbit down a hole, and falls for what seems an eternity, to arrive in strange surroundings where everything becomes "curiouser and curiouser". She drinks from a bottle labelled "DRINK ME" and shrinks. A cake marked "EAT ME" makes her grow. Her tears of frustration become a huge pool out of which she climbs in the company of other bedraggled creatures including a Duck, Dodo and Mouse.

Alice finds it impossible to " 'keep the same size for ten minutes together' " until she meets a large, cantankerous blue Caterpillar sitting on a mushroom. He tells her that one side of the mushroom will make her grow, and the other make her shrink. At last Alice regains control, but makes herself small again so as

The Mad Hatter's Tea-Party
This eccentric soirée was only inserted when Carroll adapted the book for publication.

not to frighten the people in a tiny house she comes upon.

Here she encounters the Cheshire Cat and the sneezing, brutish Duchess, whose screeching lullaby to the howling baby on her knee drives Alice in search of peace and sanity. Instead she finds the Mad Hatter's Tea-Party where he, the March Hare and dozy Dormouse are permanently locked into a six o'clock tea-time. They exasperate Alice with unanswerable riddles and nonsense, until she leaves in disgust.

She finds herself at the Queen of Hearts' garden party, where everyone is playing croquet. The mallets are live flamingoes, the balls are curled up hedgehogs, and all the guests are under constant threat of execution.

Wearying of the confusion, Alice wanders away to an encounter with the Gryphon and Mock Turtle, who show her how the Lobster Quadrille is danced and sing her a curious song. She recites a poem that comes out "very queer indeed" – she wonders if anything will "ever happen in a natural way again".

But in the distance the trial is beginning, to discover who stole the Queen of Hearts' tarts, and the Gryphon hurries Alice away to the courtroom. But she begins to grow again . . .

The sequel to *Alice in Wonderland* was published six years later. Alice is again the central character, this time moving within the structure of a chess game. She passes through a mirror into a world peopled with chessmen and nursery-rhyme characters and where everything is back-to-front. The Red Queen dubs Alice the White Queen's Pawn and explains the necessary moves to become a Queen herself.

LOOKING-GLASS COUNTRY

On her way through the squares – briefly travelling by train – she meets a gallery of characters. She encounters Tweedledum and Tweedledee in the fourth square, who proffer plenty of "contrariwise" advice and recite *The Walrus and the Carpenter*. The dithering White Queen, giddy with "living backwards", is bleatingly transformed into a shop-keeping sheep with whom Alice goes rowing.

Alice buys an egg which gradually turns into Humpty Dumpty sitting on his wall. She has a long, puzzling conversation with him and moves on, just before he crashes to the ground. The White Knight at last leads her to the safety of the final square.

FOR CHILDREN ABOVE ALL

The *Alice* books are, first and foremost, written for children. It should be remembered that *Alice in Wonderland* has its origins in a story improvised and recounted to actual children, one sunny afternoon on the Thames. Though written down and later adapted and extended, it retains all the freshness of a child-like imagination and an almost bewildering love of word-play.

Both books engage a child's imagination without moralizing. They are an exploration of mystery, nightmare and fantasy interspersed with humorous parodies of well-known verse and of language itself – all interpreted through the eyes of Alice, a bright little girl invested with a great deal of sound common sense.

The author uses the simple device of setting his fantastical events within the framework of a dream. In both books the action is explained away at the end by Alice waking, but while she dreams, anything is possible.

Sensible Alice
Naturally intrepid, Alice (above) is also blessed with common sense, which enables her to cope in the most bizarre situations.

'A pack of cards'
Not until the Queen's garden party does it become clear that the royalty of Wonderland are simply the colour cards of a well-shuffled pack.

Do-Do Dodgson
The Duck and the Dodo (left) who race with Alice originally represented the Reverend Duckworth (who was in the boat when Carroll improvised the story), and Dodgson himself, who, because of his stammer, used to introduce himself as Do-Do-Dodgson.

ses are ones which would have been known to Alice, but with different words. For example, the Duchess's lullaby:

'Speak roughly to your little boy,
And beat him when he sneezes:
He only does it to annoy,
Because he knows it teases.'

was suggested by a verse by David Bates:

'Speak gently to the little child!
Its love be sure to gain;
Teach it in accents soft and mild –
It may not long remain.'

In the Background

THE NONSENSE MAN

Lewis Carroll was well acquainted with Edward Lear's *Book of Nonsense* published in 1846. Its zany enjoyment of invented words and fantastic creatures must surely have influenced the writer of the *Jabberwocky*. And Lear must, to some extent, have paved the way for the success of *Alice*. Though primarily a serious painter, Lear is now best remembered for such verses as *The Owl and the Pussycat*.

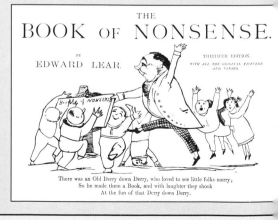

Beware the Jabberwock!

Attempts to analyze the nonsense vocabulary of this famous poem are probably futile – children understand it well enough.

Much of the tension in Alice's travels lies in never knowing what will happen next. The kindest creatures suddenly become unpredictable and hostile. She is either too big or too small. No-one seems to understand her. She feels her identity has slipped away, as she tries to explain to the contemptuous Caterpillar:

'I know who I was *when I got up this morning, but I think I must have been changed several times since then.'*

Other creatures make alarming statements in the most matter-of-fact tones. The Cheshire Cat, for example, observes:

'we're all mad here. I'm mad. You're mad.'

'How do you know I'm mad?' said Alice.

'You must be,' said the Cat, *'or you wouldn't have come here.'*

The pace of the action hardly gives Alice pause for thought. But there are enough familiar nursery-rhyme figures – Tweedledum and Tweedledee, Humpty Dumpty, the Lion and the Unicorn – to provide reassurance as well as amusement.

Some of the nonsense alludes to rhymes and games long forgotten. For instance, 'I love my love with an A' was a popular word game. Similarly, most of the poems and ver-

Edward Lear (1812-1888) was a painter, poet, illustrator of his own verse (left) and drawing master to Queen Victoria.

The second 'Alice'
Carroll had already been making up various stories about chessmen for his little cousin, Alice Raikes, when one day he invited her to his house and asked her questions about the little girl reflected in the mirror there. This was the germ of Alice Through the Looking-Glass *(left).*

Nowadays, Carroll's parodies are more famous than the poems they parodied, and the only original which children today are likely to recognize is 'Twinkle Twinkle Little Star', which the Mad Hatter parodies:

'Twinkle, Twinkle little bat!
How I wonder what you're at!'

Both books conclude with a rising crescendo of madness which Alice firmly denounces. At the end of *Alice in Wonderland*, she shouts at the Queen and courtroom, "Who cares for you?... You're nothing but a

A wistful parting
The last time Carroll made an outing with Alice Liddell, he saw she was growing up. Like the White Knight (right) he said, "I'll see you safe to the end of the wood – and then I must go back, you know. That's the end of my move."

pack of cards!' " In waking, Alice rejoins the safe 'real' world of older sisters and favourite kittens.

It is no surprise that a logician and mathematician should have made such use of word-play and 'illogical logic'. The Jabberwocky poem, for example, excited a fever of interest on publication, giving rise to a variety of 'translations', but Carroll was simply

"Then fill up the glasses
as quick as you can,
And sprinkle the table
with buttons and bran:
Put cats in the coffee,
and mice in the tea –
And welcome Queen Alice
with thirty-times-three!"

mocking the moral Victorian rhymes children were forced to learn by heart and recite to adults. Throughout the books, Carroll treads the very fine line between logic and nonsense. The dialogue slips between the two – at one moment breathtakingly simple in argument, at the next utterly nonsensical. Humpty

Dumpty, smugly serene on his wall, displays an unshakeable grasp of logic which Alice grapples with as best she can:

'Why do you sit out here all alone?' asked Alice, not wishing to begin an argument.
'Why, because there's no one with me!' cried Humpty Dumpty. 'Did you think I didn't know the answer to that? Ask another!'

It is Humpty Dumpty who instructs Alice in the usage of 'portmanteau' words which carry more than one meaning. He also points out the linguistic truth that the meaning of words is simply an attitude of mind:

'The question is,' said Alice, 'whether you can make words mean so many different things.'
'The question is,' said Humpty Dumpty, 'which is to be master – that's all.'

Scholars have delighted in constructing hidden depths of meaning in Carroll's work – all of which greatly bemused him. When questioned about a later book of his, *The Hunting of the Snark*, he said: 'I'm very much afraid I didn't mean anything but nonsense! Still, you know, words mean more than we mean to express when we use them; so a whole book ought to mean a great deal more than the writer meant. So, whatever good meanings are in the book, I'm very glad to accept as the meaning of the book.'

Alice by Arthur Rackham. With permission of Barbara Edwards, daughter of the artist

CHARACTERS IN FOCUS

Carroll invented a dazzling array of characters, all of whom would be unbelievable in any context other than Wonderland or the back-to-front world of Looking-Glass Land. Their singular remarks have become household phrases and their nonsensical poetry better known than the verse it parodies. Amid the chaos of the unexpected, the nursery-rhyme characters lend friendly reassurance. Adaptable and self-reliant, Alice remains undaunted by each new – and perplexing – encounter.

In her travels through Wonderland, Alice (left) meets a mixture of eccentric animals and playing-card people. The Looking-Glass world is peopled with chess pieces and nursery-rhyme characters.

Tweedledum and Tweedledee (above) are paragons of logic – "if it was so, it might be; and if it were so, it would be; but as it isn't, it ain't."

Humpty Dumpty (right) can explain all poems – "and a good many that haven't been invented just yet".

The King of Hearts (below) conducts a crazy Wonderland trial: "Let the jury consider their verdict," the King said . . . "No, no!" said the Queen. "Sentence first – verdict afterwards."

"Stuff and nonsense!" said Alice loudly . . . "Off with her head!"

The Red Queen rushes across the chess board – to stay in the same place.

The Cheshire Cat (above) mystifies Alice: "Well! I've often seen a cat without a grin . . . but a grin without a cat!"

Alice tries to make sense of Wonderland's characters. But the pipe-smoking Caterpillar (left) gives her contradictory advice; the talk of the Mad Hatter (above) seems "to have no sort of meaning", and the White Rabbit (below) is always in a rush.

The Walrus and the Carpenter (below) are the subjects of Tweedledee's poem – they "talk of many things:/of shoes – and ships – and sealing wax–/Of cabbages – and kings . . ."

The Duchess maintains "flamingoes and mustard both bite. And the moral of that is – 'Birds of a feather flock together.'"

"Only mustard isn't a bird," Alice remarked.

White Rabbit and Caterpillar by Arthur Rackham. With permission of Barbara Edwards, daughter of the artist.

AMATEUR OF GENIUS

Although he is regarded as one of the masters of children's fiction, Carroll made up his stories for the private entertainment of his child-friends, and never publicly acknowledged their authorship.

Children's books and poems, 'serious' works such as *Euclid and his Rivals,* mathematical puzzles, word games, pamphlets attacking vivisection, papers on logic and descriptions of inventions like the Nyctograph (for writing in the dark) – the works of Charles Lutwidge Dodgson have a randomness and variety that could only come from a literary amateur of genius. Dodgson never publicly admitted authorship of his famous children's books, and returned unanswered letters addressed to 'Lewis Carroll, Christ Church, Oxford'. He wished to retain his amateur status and his anonymity – 'to remain, *personally,* in the obscurity of a private individual'.

Carroll's earliest writings were entirely private in intention. From the age of 13 he was chief author and illustrator of a series of magazines 'published' at the Croft Rectory,

to entertain his brothers and sisters. The very first, *Useful and Instructive Poetry,* already displays a wry disrespect for solemn discourses, and a love of nonsense. His handiwork at 13 included:

> There was once a young man of Oporta
> Who daily got shorter and shorter,
> The reason he said
> Was the hod on his head
> Which was filled with the heaviest mortar.

Later, as a young Oxford Fellow, Carroll wrote some humorous pieces for *Comic Times* and *The Train.* It was the editor of these magazines, Edmund Yates, who chose 'Lewis Carroll' out of a list of possible pseudonyms provided by Dodgson. But Yates' magazines were short-lived, and Lewis Carroll's literary career effectively stood still for seven years, although C.L. Dodgson published specialist works on mathematics.

The child model
(left) Lewis Carroll took this photograph of Alice Liddell, the inspiration for his first fictional Alice.

Telling tales
(right and below) The Wonderland episodes entertained Alice Liddell during boating trips and picnics.

It is well known that *Alice in Wonderland* would never have been put down on paper except at the insistence of his 'child-friend' Alice Liddell for whom he improvised it. He began composing the book in 1862, to give it to her as a Christmas present. Encouraged by friends, Carroll decided to publish it, and in 1865 *Alice's Adventures in Wonderland* came into existence.

Through the Looking-Glass, like *Alice in Wonderland,* was inspired by a real Alice – eight-year-old Alice Raikes whom he saw while staying with his uncle, Skeffington Lutwidge, in Onslow Square, London. 'The volume' noted Dodgson, on receiving the galley proofs in January 1871, 'has cost me, I think, more trouble than the first, and *ought* to be equal to it in every way'. In terms of sales, it was never equal to the first *Alice,* but it was nevertheless a resounding success. In time, the two books came to be viewed almost as one.

IMPROVISED TALES

Carroll was a practised improviser of stories, though most 'lived and died like summer-midges, each in its own golden afternoon'. We gain a glimpse of his spontaneous method when he describes the genesis of *Alice* – 'in a desperate attempt to strike out some new line of fairy-lore, I had sent my heroine straight down a rabbit-hole, to begin with, without the least idea what was to happen afterwards'.

But this picture of casual, extemporary story-telling is misleading. It obscures the slow, piecemeal way in which Carroll actually built up his books. Many of the materials which went to make up *Alice* probably existed in Carroll's mind – even on paper – before that memorable day on the river. The verses read out by the White Rabbit at the trial of the Knave of Hearts had already appeared years before in *Comic Times.*

Carroll wrote not one, but two manuscript versions of *Alice in Wonderland* for his child-friend; and when he decided to publish, he greatly expanded the narrative. Only at this point were some of the most famous episodes inserted, including the Mad Hatter's Tea-Party and Alice's encounter with the Cheshire Cat. He also added a sophisticated layer of word-play and parody to what had been a straightforward, if surreal, adventure story. He thus transformed *Alice* into a classic that appeals as strongly to adults as to children.

Carroll himself noted that ' "Alice" and the "Looking-Glass" are made up almost wholly of bits and scraps, single ideas which came of themselves.' The poems, such as *Jabberwocky* and *The Walrus and the Carpenter,* are the most obvious examples. His was evidently a mind into which puns, nonsensical lines of verse and scraps of dialogue were constantly intruding. This was the way in which *The Hunting of the Snark* came to be written: 'I was walking on a hillside, alone, one bright summer day, when suddenly there came into my head one line of verse – one solitary line – "For the Snark *was* a Boojum, you see." I knew not what it meant, then: I know not what it means, now; but I wrote it down: and, some time after-

Illustrating Alice
Carroll even illustrated his manuscript of Alice in Wonderland for Alice Liddell. His drawings are in the accompanying book (example, right). The first published version was illustrated by John Tenniel, as was Through the Looking-Glass (centre). Tenniel's suggestions for the text (see letter, far right), were even – at times – taken up by the author.

Mansell Collection

wards, the rest of the stanza occurred to me, that being its last line: and so by degrees, at odd moments during the next year or two, the rest of the poem pieced itself together.'

Carroll had intended to include *The Hunting of the Snark* in his last children's book, *Sylvie and Bruno,* but the poem grew too long while the book grew too slowly. Originating in the story, 'Bruno's Revenge', which Carroll wrote for *Aunt Judy's Magazine* in 1867, *Sylvie and Bruno* was not completed until more than 20 years later. 'As the years went on, I jotted down, at odd moments, all sorts of odd ideas, and fragments of dialogue, that occurred to me – who knows how?'

In fact, Carroll did trace such 'random flashes of thought' to his reading, to friends' chance remarks and to dreams. For example Tennyson once recounted a dream in which he studied a 'shaped' poem: the opening lines were long and the closing lines very short indeed. Although Tennyson could not remember the substance of the poem after he woke up, Carroll, when he wrote 'The Mouse's Tale' in *Alice in Wonderland,* clearly remembered Tennyson's dream.

In the case of *Sylvie and Bruno,* Carroll's 'amateurish' piecemeal method of composition eventually put him in possession of a 'huge unwieldy mass' of incidents which needed only a storyline to string them together into a book. 'Only! The task, at first, seemed absolutely hopeless...and it must have been ten years, or more, before I had succeeded in classifying these odds and ends sufficiently to see what sort of a story they indicated: for the story had to grow out of the incidents, not the incidents out of the story.'

AT HIS OWN PACE

Like many authors, Carroll believed that his particular method was the only good one. There is a note of condescension and disdain when he refers to the poor professional, compelled to produce regular amounts to earn his bread. No doubt, says Carroll, in the preface to *Sylvie and Bruno,* he too could write a story straight off 'if I were in the unfortunate position...of being obliged to produce a given amount of fiction in a given time...I could "fulfil my task", and produce my "tale of bricks", as other slaves have done.' The result, however, would be 'commonplace' and 'very weary reading'. The serial-writing slaves he so disparaged of course included Dickens and Thackeray!

In writing the *Alice* stories and *The Snark,*

THE PHANTOM DANCERS QUADRILLE,

ON FAVORITE MELODIES BY ALFRED MELLON,
From the highly Successfull Burlesque, performed at the Adelphi Theatre, arranged by

JULLIEN.

T. STA. HALL.

Pr. DUETTS

"The Lobster Quadrille"
(left) In the famous dance scene in Alice in Wonderland *– "See how eagerly the lobsters and the turtles all advance!/ They are waiting on the shingle – will you come and join the dance?/ Will you, won't you, will you, won't you, will you join the dance?" – Carroll takes delightful fictional liberties with one of the most popular Victorian dances.*

"Alice's Evidence"
(right) There was a vogue in Victorian fiction for mocking the long-winded, tedious legal system. Lewis Carroll concludes Alice in Wonderland *with a ridiculous trial scene, but he was probably less interested in directly attacking the law than in rounding off the action in an appropriately fantastic way.*

Carroll promoted the trend away from morally didactic children's books towards sheer enjoyment. But strangely enough, in later years, he reverted to the traditional Victorian approach and included religious and moral reflections in his work. In *Sylvie and Bruno* he 'introduced, along with...acceptable nonsense for children, some of the graver thoughts of human life'.

The religious element takes over long sections of the second volume. The swift transitions of time and place are strikingly original and modern, but in other respects it is a thoroughly 'improving' book. The fairy and nonsense elements clash strangely with the moral dilemma of the heroine, who is promised in marriage to a godless man.

Carroll, so original a master of language, was at least a thoroughly conventional man – and writer – in most other respects. His serious poems are not unlike those that he himself parodied earlier in *How doth the little crocodile* and *You are old, Father William*.

He applied the principle of 'sugaring the pill' to teaching mathematics to children, ad-

mitting as much in his preface to his compilation puzzle book, *A Tangled Tale*: 'The writer's intention was to embody in each Knot (like the medicine so dextrously, but ineffectually, concealed in the jam of our early childhood) one or more mathematical questions – in Arithmetic, Algebra, or Geometry, as the case might be – for the amusement, and possible edification, of the fair readers...'

Thanks to his financial independence, Carroll was able to exercise considerable control over the form in which his works appeared. He himself admitted that his publisher, Macmillan's, had to endure endless questions and admonitions – 'the pelting of the pitiless storm' – until each book appeared in the shops. *Alice in Wonderland* was originally published at Carroll's expense, but when the illustrator, John Tenniel, complained about the quality of the reproductions, Carroll insisted on scrapping the entire first printing and having the work done all over again.

The self-same perfectionism made relations with his illustrators fraught. He and Tenniel parted company by mutual consent when the

second *Alice* was finished, and Harry Furniss, who illustrated *Sylvie and Bruno*, wrote of Carroll: 'He would take a square inch of the drawing, count the lines I had made in that space...And in the course I would receive a long essay on the subject from Dodgson the mathematician.' In reality, Carroll's pernickety nature operated in his illustrators' own best interests. Under his guidance, their drawings became so closely integrated with the texts that they have never been replaced by later competitors. Tenniel and the rest are today remembered chiefly for their connection with the obscure, inspired, literary amateur of Christ Church, Oxford, who sometimes called himself 'Lewis Carroll'.

" —— you know you say things are 'much of a muchness'; did you ever see such a thing as a drawing of a muchness ? "
! *Alice in Wonderland*.

ALICE AND THE DORMOUSE.

Marsell Collection

Stage and song
(right) Alice's Adventures in Wonderland *was so popular that it was adapted for the stage by Savile Clarke in 1887. When writing these stories Carroll never envisaged that this would happen, nor that they would be set to music (below left).*

The Alice cult
(below right) The Alice *stories were such a success that there was a variety of spin-offs soon after their publication. Alice and the Red Queen, with Tweedledee and Tweedledum make for a marvellously colourful Looking-Glass biscuit tin.*

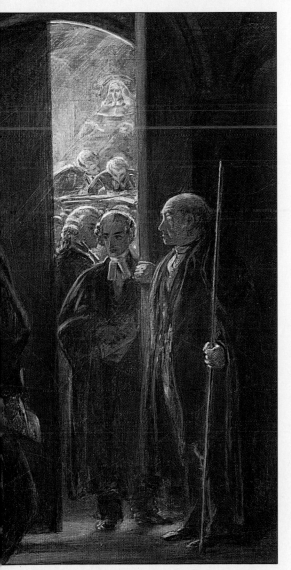

No. 18.   EMPIRE MUSIC ALBUMS.   Price 6d.

Twenty Children's Humorous Songs
The Words Selected from

ALICE IN WONDERLAND

The Music composed by
Annie C. Armstrong

LONDON: HART & CO. 22 PATERNOSTER RO

ALICE & THE RED QUEEN.

TWEEDLEDEE & TWEEDLEDUM.

Guildford Muniment Room

WORKS·IN OUTLINE

Although he wrote on many subjects, Charles Dodgson's fame rests on the books he published as Lewis Carroll – no mention is made here of the mathematical and theological writings he published under his real name. Only the wonderfully absurd epic poem, *The Hunting of the Snark* has rivalled the *Alice* books in popularity, but the poems in *Phantasmagoria* also display Carroll's dazzling manipulation of parody, puns, wordplay and nonsense.

These elements of Carroll's genius are also evident in *Sylvie and Bruno*, although these have been underrated, perhaps because the fairy-fun is intertwined with conventional Victorian sentiment. In *A Tangled Tale*, Dodgson the mathematician combines with Carroll the master of fantasy to create riddles of imaginative arithmetic for children.

SYLVIE AND BRUNO
◆ 1889 ◆

Sylvie and Bruno (right) inhabit no less than three parallel worlds. On the everyday plane, Arthur Forester, a doctor, is disappointed in his love for Lady Muriel Orme, already engaged to Eric Lindon. The narrator, meanwhile, has intermittent dreamlike experiences of Outland – a parallel, outlandish world where nonsense abounds. Its ruler, the Warden, is usurped, and his children, Sylvie and Bruno, are disinherited. The Warden, however, becomes king of a third world, Fairyland, and is joined there by his children. Sylvie is Lady Muriel's double, and so influences the events of the first, 'real' world. In some respects, these books are Carroll's most original works, because of their complex creation of interrelated worlds. But they also have elements of typical Victorian melodrama.

In *Sylvie and Bruno Concluded,* Lindon's lack of religious principles makes Muriel unwilling to marry him, and he releases her. She marries the doctor, but an epidemic threatens their happiness . . .

A TANGLED TALE
◆ 1885 ◆

Strange characters such as the 'martyr of science' (left), who illustrates the law of displacement by immersing himself in the sea (and drowning), people these tales. The stories each contain a mathematical riddle or 'Knot', which tests the reader's facility with arithmetic, algebra and geometry, by way of knights running cross-country, some refined train-spotters, a treasure lost overboard, a visit to a picture gallery, and a lady stuck in the door of a hansom cab. The sage character of Balbus surfaces several times, as do his pupils, Hugh and Lambert. Carroll's favourite pastime of pursuing a line of reasoning to its ultimate (illogical) conclusion is in evidence, too, and is highly diverting. The solutions to the ten 'Knots' are given in daunting detail at the end.

A Tangled Tale is now usually presented with *Pillow Problems* – 72 mathematical puzzles worked out by Carroll 'while lying awake at night' or 'while taking a solitary walk'. They are certainly not for any ordinary kind of child, nor for the intellectually feeble, as sines and cosines feature more strongly than fun.

Illustration hand tinted by Graham Bingham

THE HUNTING OF THE SNARK
◆ 1876 ◆

The Bellman, Billiard-maker, Banker, Barrister, Bonnet-maker and Baker (with seven coats) are among the ten-creature crew (left) – all Bs – that set sail in pursuit of the Snark. In this epic poem, subtitled 'An Agony in Eight Fits', the Bellman-captain navigates by a map that shows only the sea (and is therefore blank) and issues orders no-one can understand. But he does know the 'five unmistakable marks' by which 'warranted, genuine Snarks' are known. These are the Snark's crispy taste, its habit of rising late, its lack of humour, its fondness for bathing machines, and its ambitious nature. Unfortunately, there are several *types* of Snark, and the Baker recalls his uncle's words: "beware of the day,/If your Snark be a Boojum!" After encounters with the Jubjub bird and Bandersnatch of *Jabberwocky* fame, the Snark is finally tracked down and the awful truth of its nature revealed. The poem's last, nonsensical line was Carroll's creative starting point.

PHANTASMAGORIA
AND OTHER POEMS
◆ 1869 ◆

The little Sprite (above) who sets about haunting the narrator of the title poem has come to the wrong house, but it takes him seven cantos to find this out and leave in search of the correct victim. In the meantime, we have been instructed in the tribulations and regulations governing the lives of ghosts who go a-haunting.

All the poems are comic, and include a delightful parody of Longfellow's *Hiawatha*, in which Carroll pokes fun at photographers like himself. An interminable Scottish ballad, complete with dialect spelling, tells the sad story of "The Lang Coortin" of a kilted suitor who is eventually laughed out of court by the lady's raucous popinjay (left).

'A Moment in Time'

The ability to capture the moment came about with the invention of photography in the mid-19th century. But like much Victorian painting, it was often used to evoke the poetry of bygone days.

O n the last page of the original manuscript of *Alice's Adventures in Wonderland* is pasted a tiny photograph of the real Alice: Alice Liddell. Charles Dodgson – alias Lewis Carroll – took the picture himself, and it is just one of many he took of her. Carroll was a dedicated photographer – now regarded as one of the greatest of all Victorian photographers. And during the long, warm summer days of her childhood, Alice and her sisters would often pose for hours for 'Mr Dodgson' while he adjusted his camera and attempted to entrance them with his whimsical, delightful stories. Photography concentrated his imaginative interests in more ways than one.

From 1856 until July 1880 – a period during which photographic principles and techniques made many revolutionary leaps forward – Carroll's fascination with photography deepened. There were times when he would spend many hours every day behind his massive plate camera, or in the darkroom preparing the plates. Like many mid-Victorians with an eye on posterity and the future, he was keen to include his heroes in his photograph album, and many famous people – such as Prince Leopold, the painters John Everett Millais and Dante Gabriel Rossetti, and the scientist Michael Faraday – became his subjects.

PHOTOGRAPHIC ORDEAL

When Carroll bought his first camera, in March 1856, photography was a comparatively young art, still exciting and rather mysterious. It was less than 17 years before, in August 1839, that the details of Louis Daguerre's momentous discovery had been revealed to an excited audience at the French Academie des Sciences. And it was barely 12 years since William Henry Fox Talbot had patented his 'calotype' process, the first practical process to use a negative.

The phenomenon of photography had caught on quickly, and before long thousands of middle-class Victorians were willingly subjecting themselves to the ordeal of posing for a daguerreotype portrait. That it was an ordeal is reflected in the grim faces staring out from daguerreotypes of the 1840s – hardly surprising since exposures could last many minutes, and often the only way the photographer could keep his sitter's head immobile was to clamp the neck rigidly in a vice.

Yet though many people were sitting for photographs, very few in England were actually taking them. The complexity of the process was one obstacle, but so too was the sheer cost. For besides buying very expensive materials, English photographers had to pay Daguerre a high fee for the right to use the process. This put the process beyond the reach of all but a few gifted, but more importantly, wealthy, professionals. Fox Talbot's calotype was cheaper, and had the advantage that multiple copies of a photograph could be made because the process started with a negative –

Gernsheim Collection

BBC Hulton Picture Library

Museum of the History of Science Oxford University

Carroll the photographer

(left) Lewis Carroll took up photography in 1856, and became one of the best child photographers of the 19th century. The equipment he used is shown below.

Inspired by art

(right) Like many photographers, Carroll was greatly influenced by Pre-Raphaelite portraits of 'other-worldly' young women. He owned this painting – The Lady with Lilacs by Arthur Hughes – and based an early Alice illustration on it.

The Lady with the Lilacs by Arthur Hughes, Art Gallery of Ontario, Toronto: Presented in memory of Francis Banes, Membership Secretary (1951-64) by members of Council, Women's Committee and staff of the Gallery, 1966

unlike the daguerreotype, which was a one-off. But Fox Talbot hedged his patent with so many restrictions that few bothered to take it up.

The breakthrough came in 1851, when Frederick Scott Archer launched the collodion or wet-plate process which, like the calotype, gave a negative. But it was only a lawsuit in February 1855 that persuaded Fox Talbot to relinquish his claim that the process was merely a variation of his. From then on, photography progressed in leaps and bounds, and soon thousands of well-to-do Victorians were, like Lewis Carroll, buying cameras and becoming 'pilgrims of the sun'.

Photography was still by no means simple, for the plate for each picture had to be specially prepared in a darkroom moments before use. The collodion process was messy, for the wet-plate was literally wet, and inky black stains from the chemicals on fingers and clothes earned the wet-plate process the name of 'the black art'. It could be dangerous, too. A visitor calling on the photographer Julia Margaret Cameron found her sons marching her up and down, afraid that deadly potassium cyanide might have invaded a cut on her finger.

As if all this were not enough, taking pictures anywhere but at home meant carrying around a huge photographic outfit: large bottles of chemicals, various dishes, scales, weights and measures, heavy glass plates

Naked innocence

(left) The Red and White Roses by Julia Margaret Cameron, one of the greatest 19th-century photographers, illustrates the Victorian interest in evocative portraits of naked children who belong to a lost world of purity and innocence.

In the vice

Having your photograph taken in the mid-19th century was an ordeal. To ensure that the subjects remained still for the duration of the exposure, photographers often locked them in vices – a custom satirized in this contemporary cartoon.

Mary Evans Picture Library

St. Marks, Venice by John Bunney By permission of Sheffield City Art Galleries

The art of perfection
(left) There was a strong, two-way relationship between painting and photography in the late 19th century. Highly finished paintings such as this beautiful picture of St Mark's Square, Venice by John Bunney reveal an almost photographic realism. At the same time, photographers often emulated narrative painters by making their pictures 'tell a story'.

and a vast darkroom tent – not to mention a huge plate camera and a tripod to support it. Photographers and their paraphernalia became the target for many cartoonists, and in his parody of Longfellow's poem *Hiawatha's Photographing* even Carroll pokes fun at the rigmarole of photography:

> *From his shoulder Hiawatha*
> *Took the camera of rosewood,*
> *Made of sliding, folding rosewood;*
> *Neatly put it all together.*
> *In its case it lay compactly,*
> *Folded into nearly nothing;*
> *But he opened out the hinges,*
> *Pushed and pulled the joints and hinges,*
> *Till it looked all squares and oblongs,*
> *Like a complicated figure*
> *In the Second Book of Euclid.*

> *This he perched upon a tripod -*
> *Crouched beneath its dusty cover –*
> *Stretched his hand, enforcing silence -*
> *Said, "Be motionless, I beg you!"*
> *Mystic, awful was the process.*

But none of this complexity deterred the thousands up and down the country who took up photography for business or pleasure. Now that photographs were cheap enough for even the working class to afford, the portrait business boomed. In London, Regent Street alone had 35 'glass houses' where people could have their photographs taken, and in every town in England there were photographers offering to, as *Punch* quipped, 'Take off yer 'ead for sixpence, or yer 'ole body for a shillin!'

The turnover in these portrait studios was phenomenal, and some photographers would pride themselves on the number of clients they could handle, taking as many as 100 negatives in a day for the miniature *carte-de-visite* prints that everyone wanted. Naturally, poses were stereotyped, and pictures were heavily retouched to flatter the sitter. Studios would keep on

hand a small range of popular props and backdrops to set the scene, and the results were often bizarre: women in evening dress pose inches from a wild sea-shore or rushing Alpine cataract, or men lean uncertainly against a fake Corinthian column standing alone in an Italianate landscape. Such effects were immensely popular.

Amateur photographers, meanwhile, stood aloof from this hectic business. Indeed, they sneered at it, and photographic journals of the late 1850s are full of complaints about the lamentable standards of contemporary English photography. Amateurs such as Carroll – who took pictures for pleasure, not profit – regarded photography as an art form and took it, and themselves, extremely seriously.

BATTLE OF THE ARTS

One of the many thorny problems for the amateur was that they were not quite sure what direction such an art should take. They were also acutely sensitive to criticism that photography was not an art at all, but merely a mechanical process. Painters were especially likely to make this gibe, for they were equally sensitive to the suggestion that photography made painting redundant – particularly as the invention of photography had actually put hundreds of portrait painters out of business.

Paradoxically, though, both photographers and the young Pre-Raphaelite painters, such as John Everett Millais and William Holman Hunt, had pursued the same ideal in the 1850s: to render Nature in ever more realistic detail. The foxgloves and nettles, ivy and dockleaves that Millais and Hunt painted in exquisite detail, were now photographed with equal sharpness.

The rivalry between painters and photographers was often intense. Photographers crowed that Millais could be 'beat...hollow' by photography and that Francis Bedford's photographs of plants 'would set a Pre-Raphaelite crazy.' The Pre-Raphaelites were equally disparaging about photographers. Indeed, they were extremely touchy about being linked with photo-

Artistic composition
(below and right) Just as paintings could be based on photographs, so photographic compositions could be as carefully planned as an oil painting. The photograph Carolling *by H.P. Robinson was initially composed in a sketch (right), before being set up.*

Victor a and Albert Museum

Reverie by D. G. Rossetti: Christie's, London Bridgeman Art Library

Royal Photographic Society

Pre-Raphaelite models

Both photographers and painters associated with the Pre-Raphaelites created portraits of women with pensive, idealized beauty. Dante Gabriel Rossetti oversaw this photograph (above left) of his adored Jane Morris (wife of William Morris) at a sitting in his Chelsea home in 1865. The portrait, taken by the professional photographer John R. Parsons became the basis of Rossetti's painting Reverie *(above).*

graphy at all, mainly for fear critics might suggest they painted over photographs.

Nevertheless, photographers remained acutely sensitive to the accusation that photography was incapable of high art – an accusation reinforced by the boom in cheap portrait photography. Disillusioned by the struggle to achieve ever greater detail and 'truth to nature', which seemed a purely scientific problem, many photographers sought a way of turning photography into a genuine art form.

In the late 1850s, a number of photographers, such as Oscar Rejlander and Henry Peach Robinson, began to tackle pointedly 'artistic' subjects. They built up elaborate, painterly pictures with a story or moral, by joining together staged photographs of models in costume. Rejlander's vast Renaissance-style tableau called 'The Two Ways of Life' (1857) was a great success, and was purchased by Queen Victoria herself, while Robinson's touching deathbed scene entitled 'Fading Away' became one of the most popular of all Victorian photographs. Such pictures appealed to Victorian taste for morality and melodrama and, for the next 20 years, reproductions of similar 'artistic' photographs sold in considerable numbers. Peter Henry Emerson went one step further – he took his camera into the fields and fens to 'capture' highly stylized naturalistic pictures. But

51

Royal Photographic Society

later, in proclaiming that photography was not Art, he set in motion a debate that raged into the next century. Robinson and others rose to the challenge and sought to develop 'the highest form of art of which photography is capable.'

Lewis Carroll met both Rejlander and Robinson, and was especially drawn to Rejlander's pictures of children in costume. But about the time he was writing *Alice in Wonderland,* in the early 1860s, he began to mix in a circle of people who were creating a new mood in the art world – a circle including such celebrities as the poet Tennyson, the Pre-Raphaelite painters Hunt, Millais, Rossetti and Arthur Hughes, and the photographers David Wilkie Wynfield and Julia Margaret Cameron, perhaps the greatest of all Victorian photographers.

Within this circle, the concern for realism had given way to an obsession with Beauty, and at Little Holland House in London, Sarah Prinsep (like Julia Cameron, one of the famous Pattle sisters) and the painter G.F. Watts created an ambience conducive to the discussion of the Beautiful. There was little sense of time in this house, and young women in loose, flowing dresses and long, wild hair would float in and out, while the men dreamed of bygone ages, painted and photographed.

Neither the painters nor photographers of this circle were now so interested in capturing realistic detail. Julia Margaret Cameron even took pictures out of focus. What they were concerned with was Beauty and 'poetry' and, in particular, inner, spiritual beauty. For many men, dreamy women with long, flowing hair represented the ideal. Their dreaminess suggested spirituality, and young women with a distant look were popular subjects for both painters such as Rossetti and photographers like Julia Margaret Cameron.

Carroll was never very comfortable in the Little Holland House set, or with its ideas. But he shared the wistful concern of the circle for fragile young beauty. He felt that the tender beauty of young girls faded as they left childhood behind them. It was little girls like Alice Liddell and Xie Kitchin – rather than young women – that he sought out as subjects for his photographs. Sometimes, he was content to photograph them as they arrived, dressed in ordinary clothes. But often he felt that these clothes obscured the innocent beauty of his young subjects, and he would dress them in white flannel nightgowns or, occasionally, photograph them without any clothes at all. 'Naked children are so perfectly pure and lovely' he wrote.

He longed to enter the dreamworld of his young friends – a dreamworld like Alice's – and many of his photographs have a dreamy, distant look about them. But he knew that this dreamworld, and along with it the vulnerable beauty, would be lost as the child grew. His photographs, like his books, recaptured a fragment of that lost time.

Fine-art photography
As photography came to be acknowledged as an art form, a vogue arose for 'artistic' photographic prints. One of the most popular prints to adorn Victorian walls was Gathering Waterlilies *by P.H. Emerson (above). Its peaceful atmosphere belies the messy and sometimes hazardous wet-plate or collodion process by which it was produced. Among the chemicals in which the photographic plate was drenched was the deadly potassium cyanide.*

EVELYN WAUGH

↤ *1903-1966* ↦

Evelyn Waugh was a quirky genius who came to revel in his
public image of 'eccentric don and testy colonel'. Beneath the
mask was a serious artist of great integrity and discipline, a writer
who created hilarious anarchy from the most exquisitely precise
prose. He made his name as a satirist of upper-class society, while
later novels drew on his travel and war experiences. Waugh
believed that novelists should provide entertainment which he
did by crafting novels of timeless comedy.

AGAINST THE TIDE

Although for a time Waugh entered into the party spirit of the modern age, he was an intensely conservative man, both suspicious and disdainful of the world around him.

Like his fictional self-portrait, Gilbert Pinfold, Evelyn Waugh's "strongest tastes were negative. He abhorred plastics, Picasso, sunbathing, and jazz – everything, in fact, that had happened in his own lifetime." Waugh was a snob and a pessimist, convinced that all change was for the worse. He was also extremely sensitive, prone to self-hatred and despair, a perfectionist who fell short of his own ideals. His renowned rudeness, and the reactionary views he flaunted, were often 'half facetious' – his way of dealing with what seemed an increasingly chaotic world. Waugh purposely made it near impossible for anyone to glimpse the man behind the mask.

He was born in London's West Hampstead on 28 October 1903, the second son of Arthur and Catherine Waugh. Four years later the family moved up the hill to an Edwardian villa called 'Underhill', between Hampstead village and Golders Green. Waugh often expressed regret that he was not born into the aristocracy. Arthur Waugh was a minor literary figure, a reviewer and editor, and managing director of a publishing company. Waugh's mother was descended from the eminent judge Lord Cockburn. He loved her

devotedly in childhood, as he did his nurse Lucy Hodges. His father's rather sentimental nature, however, did not find favour with Waugh, and their relationship was often uneasy.

By his own account, Waugh's childhood was unremarkable and 'lyrically happy'. The outbreak of World War I stirred him to early patriotism – he sold jam jars to raise funds for the Red Cross and with friends formed a gang called Pistol Troop for 'the defence of the kingdom'. Artistic as well as typically boyish, he wrote stories, kept diaries and drew pictures.

In 1917 Waugh went to Lancing College on the edge of the South Downs in Sussex. His early days there were 'black misery'. 'That awful little tick, Waugh' was never popular. He was short, plump and bespectacled. The Gothic chapel held more attractions for him than the playing fields, and although he would have liked 'to be accepted as one of this distasteful mob' he found it impossible to conform. He was arrogant and conceited, and to court popularity became a 'Bolshie', playing practical jokes and affecting a generally rebellious air. In the classroom, however, he excelled and came away with many academic prizes.

Lancing College

Lancing College
Waugh flourished academically at school, but was miserably lonely. The school chapel was his 'refuge'.

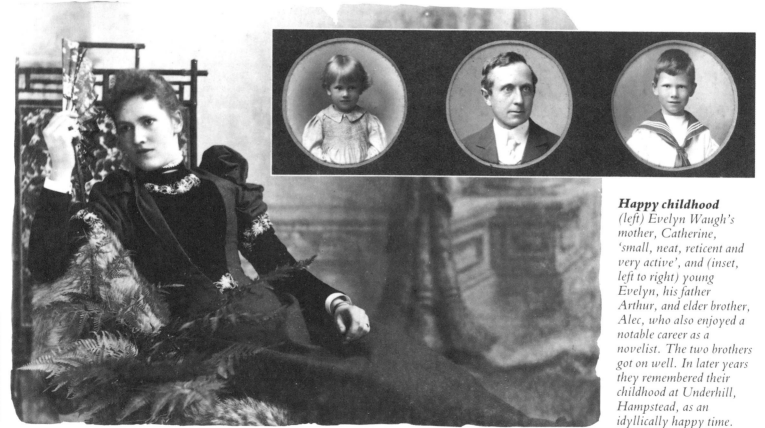

Happy childhood
(left) Evelyn Waugh's mother, Catherine, 'small, neat, reticent and very active', and (inset, left to right) young Evelyn, his father Arthur, and elder brother, Alec, who also enjoyed a notable career as a novelist. The two brothers got on well. In later years they remembered their childhood at Underhill, Hampstead, as an idyllically happy time.

'War work'
(right) This 1916 diary entry records the young Waugh doing his bit for the war effort, by 'cutting out soles for soldiers' shoes'. 'All the same', he adds, 'I think I shall chuck it soon as it cuts into the holls . . .'

Living it up
(below) Waugh poses on Queensbury, his new motor-bicycle, on Magdalen Bridge, Oxford, in 1925. Though he was no longer a student, he continued the riotous living of his undergraduate days.

Two men – he called them his 'mentors' – exerted great influence on Waugh in his Lancing years. His French teacher J. F. Roxburgh impressed Waugh with his worldly sophistication, while Francis Crease appealed to another side of his character. Crease was 'a neuter, evasive, hypochondriacal recluse' who taught the ancient art of illuminating manuscripts. Though Waugh was quickly to outgrow his admiration of these two figures, they represented contradictory impulses in himself – the man-of-the-world versus the artist – that he never fully resolved.

From Lancing, Waugh went on to Hertford College, Oxford, in 1922. His first two terms there were the lull before the storm. There followed a period of riotous, dissipated living that started with his introduction to the Hypocrites Club, a club whose members were notorious for their drunkenness and flamboyance of dress. Waugh held wild dinner parties, had homosexual affairs, drank to excess and made a big show of behaving obnoxiously and rowdily. 'Why do you have to make such a noise?', he was asked. 'Because I'm poor,' he replied. He ran up large debts trying to hold his own with aristocratic and gilded youths like Harold Acton and Hugh Lygon. 'Quite broke and rather stupid and quite incredibly depraved morally', Waugh left Oxford in June 1924 with a poor third class degree in Modern History and little idea of where his life would lead.

His diaries describe the period 1924-28 as 'a record of continuous failure'. Though he had had stories and articles published in university magazines he saw his future in lettering and drawing. But after a disillusioning spell at an art school in London and an aborted plan to become apprenticed to a print maker, financial considerations forced him to take a teaching post in North Wales. He had entered the unhappiest period of his life.

When he could, he drank and partied as much as

He- and She-Evelyn
(above) The breakdown of his first marriage to Evelyn Gardner – after she had fallen in love with another man – came as a complete shock to Waugh. Until then he had thought them a 'serenely happy' couple. For two painful weeks they tried to patch up the marriage, to no avail. 'Evelyn was not an affectionate person. I was', wrote She-Evelyn many years later.

Remote places
(right) Foreign travel inspired much of Waugh's writing. In 1934 he holed himself up in a hotel in Morocco to work on the first half of his fourth novel, A Handful of Dust.

ever with his old Oxford set and with the Bright Young People of the 1920s. On one occasion he was fined 15s 6d for being drunk in charge of a car and his diaries record orgies and pranks with toilet seats.

But he was sickening of such excesses. He began to suffer from the insomnia that was to plague him for the rest of his life. He hated his teaching job and fell into a deep depression over his love for Olivia Plunket Greene 'of the great goo-goo eyes', the sister of an Oxford crony. And when a possible job in Italy fell through he decided on desperate measures – he would kill himself.

TURNING POINT
We have a jellyfish to thank for Waugh's literary legacy. As he swam out to sea under a full moon, intent on drowning, he was stung, literally, back to his senses. In pain, but also very much alive, he returned to the shore. Later he took another teaching post, at what he termed 'a school for backward peers', Aston Clinton, in Buckinghamshire. A typical diary entry reads, 'Taught lunatics. Played rugby football. Drank at Bell.'

He lasted at Aston Clinton until the beginning of 1927, when he was sacked for the combined sins of drinking and trying to seduce a matron. It was then that he decided that life might be better as 'a man of letters.'

Seven months later he was finishing off a biography of the painter Dante Gabriel Rossetti, and his first novel, *Decline and Fall*, was well under way. He was also falling in love with Evelyn

Gardner, a bright and vivacious former debutante. He proposed to her over dinner at the Ritz, and on 27 June 1928 they married quietly and secretly in London. The publication of *Rossetti: His Life and Works* had already signalled Waugh's arrival on the literary scene. *Decline and Fall* came out in September, to great acclaim, as the newlyweds were settling into a small flat in Islington. Waugh could not have been happier.

Just eight months later, however, the marriage had broken down and Waugh's world had fallen apart. 'I did not know it was possible to be so miserable and live', he wrote to Harold Acton. Waugh's divorce, on the grounds of She-Evelyn's adultery with an old Etonian, was granted in June 1930. Three months later Waugh entered the Roman Catholic Church.

FOREIGN TRAVELS

The failure of Waugh's marriage was a watershed in his life and work. It hastened his conversion to Roman Catholicism, a major influence from this time on. It also triggered a new bitterness and misanthropy in him that intensified as he grew older. And it left him, without a domestic anchor, free to travel extensively for the next seven years.

In November 1930, as foreign correspondent for *The Times*, he attended the coronation in Addis Ababa of Emperor Haile Selassie of Ethiopia. He journeyed widely in Africa, a trip that yielded the travel book *Remote People* and his third novel *Black Mischief*. In 1935 he covered the colonial conflict between Italy and Abyssinia for the *Daily Mail*.

CATHOLICISM

For Waugh, the Church of Rome represented tradition, civilized values and good taste – qualities he found increasingly lacking in the world around him. Although he claimed that 'from sixteen to twenty-eight I didn't go to church at all', he was always devout. His decision to convert to Roman Catholicism following the break-up of his first marriage was, typically, based 'on firm intellectual conviction'. But could a man capable of Waugh's unprovoked rudeness and cruelty still be a Christian and a practising Catholic? Nancy Mitford once put the question to him after his jibes had reduced a dinner guest to tears. 'You have no idea', he replied, 'how much nastier I would be if I was not a Catholic.'

On his way back to London from this assignment he was granted an interview with the Fascist leader Mussolini in Rome. Waugh always delighted in going against the grain, and paid naïve tribute to Mussolini's brutal imperialism in *Waugh in Abyssinia*. He also found himself in a minority in his support for Franco and the Nationalist cause during the Spanish Civil War.

Many people found such allegiances unpalatable, but his growing celebrity earned him many admirers among the fashionable social

Lady Diana Cooper
(above) Lady Diana Cooper, famous society beauty, captivated Waugh with her wit and sophistication, and they developed a warm friendship. She was the model for Mrs Stitch in Scoop – *a portrait that delighted her.*

The Hollywood treatment
Waugh would not agree to Brideshead Revisited being treated as a love story on the big screen – but he and his second wife Laura were entertained lavishly on their visit to California in 1947. He became intrigued by the burial rites at Forest Lawn Cemetery and returned there day after day. It inspired The Loved One.

Fact or Fiction

ROSA LEWIS

Waugh peopled his novels with many characters drawn from real life. In *Vile Bodies* the owner of Shepheard's Hotel, Lottie Crump, "a fine figure of a woman", is a direct portrait of Rosa Lewis (inset), complete with her two cairn terriers. She ran the Cavendish Hotel (below), one of Waugh's drinking haunts, in London's Jermyn Street. (She also inspired the British television series, *The Duchess of Duke Street*.) Waugh also borrowed the name of one of her staff, her aged maître d'hotel, for the vulgar social climber, Archie Schwert. Outraged by her portrayal in *Vile Bodies,* Rosa Lewis barred the 'bastard', 'that little swine Evelyn Waugh' from ever setting foot in the Cavendish Hotel again.

circles. And he was falling in love again. Laura Herbert – ironically, a cousin of his first wife – was 21 when she and Waugh married in London in April 1937. They may have seemed an ill-matched couple – he loud and opinionated, she quiet and reserved – but their marriage, and their six children, brought them great contentment. They lived at Piers Court in Gloucestershire, and later at Combe Florey in Somerset.

Shortly after the outbreak of World War II Waugh joined the Royal Marines as a second lieutenant. He served in Africa and joined the Commandos under Colonel Bob Laycock, with whom he fought in the battle for Crete in 1941. He spent the next two years back in England and saw out the war in Yugoslavia.

The tradition of the officer and gentleman naturally appealed to Waugh, but he made a poor soldier. With his snobbish distaste for those not born to privilege he could not get on with the men in his charge. A fellow officer recorded that 'he bullied them. He bewildered them purposely'. On one occasion his Colonel even placed a sentry outside Waugh's tent to guard against one of his own men trying to kill him while he slept. Waugh's bravery and humour were invaluable assets, however. The terrifying aerial bombardment of the Allied forces on Crete, his first experience of battle, he dismissed with typical composure as being 'like German opera, too long and too loud'.

He completed two novels during the war years, *Put Out More Flags* and *Brideshead Revisited* – the latter an enormous success. In 1947 he and Laura spent a month in Hollywood, courtesy of MGM, to discuss a possible film of *Brideshead*. The film came to nothing, but the trip enabled him to visit Forest Lawn Cemetery where he 'found a deep mine of literary gold' that yielded up his next novel, the gruesomely funny *The Loved One*.

WITHDRAWAL FROM THE WORLD
Waugh had been dismayed by the push for social change signalled by the Labour Party's overwhelming election victory in 1945. He refused to vote in elections on the grounds of what he called 'conscientious objection to parliamentary democracy'. He complemented this intense conservatism by wearing loud check suits in parody of the country squire. From this time on his diaries record a withdrawal from the world.

If Waugh had his critics, he could also command intense loyalty in friends. In those post-war years guests at his West Country 'squiredom', and at his club in London, White's, included the poet John Betjeman and the novelist Graham Greene. With his socialist sympathies, Greene would not seem a natural companion for Waugh, yet their friendship – based largely on their shared religion – lasted until the end of his life.

The first two novels of Waugh's War Trilogy, *Men at Arms* and *Officers and Gentlemen*, were published in 1952 and 1955. By this time Waugh's constant drinking and the use of powerful sleeping draughts had taken their toll. He suffered from deafness and impaired memory and seemed older than his years. Waugh had spent much of his life feeling persecuted, but now such feelings assumed the proportions of persecution mania.

After agreeing to be interviewed for the BBC, he regarded the resultant programme as a malign conspiracy against him. He suspected friends of disloyalty, confused names and events and became alarmed by the state of his mind. As a rest cure, he set sail for Ceylon in January 1954 aboard a small cruise ship, bound, though he did not know it, for a 'sharp but brief attack of insanity'.

A TORMENTED MIND

The letters Laura Waugh received from him during this cruise alarmed her deeply. He claimed he was being plagued day and night by disembodied voices that mocked and abused him. He believed it to be the work of evil spirits. On his return to London he immediately demanded a priest to come and exorcise him of the devils that tormented his mind.

The psychiatrist summoned to his hotel that night diagnosed acute poisoning – Waugh's auditory hallucinations had been brought on by prolonged abuse of sleep-inducing drugs and alcohol. At the suggestion of the psychiatrist he now set to work on *The Ordeal of Gilbert Pinfold*.

The opening chapter of this novel, published in 1957, is a ruthless self-portrait of Waugh in his later years, a blimpish figure, besieged in his country retreat by a rapidly changing world. Waugh himself refused to use the telephone and sported an old-fashioned ear-trumpet that he once ostentatiously lowered when Malcolm Muggeridge rose to speak at a literary luncheon. (Ann Fleming, wife of the novelist Ian, cured him of using this intimidating device, by banging it sharply with a spoon as he held it to his ear.) In May 1959 he was offered the CBE, but turned it down apparently because he believed he was worthy of a higher honour.

He became increasingly melancholic and lethargic. The publication, in 1961, of the concluding volume of the *Sword of Honour*, *Unconditional Surrender*, marked the end of his career as a novelist. The 'prancing faun', as Harold Acton had described him at Oxford, was now corpulent and florid, worried by his rotting teeth, plagued by insomnia. He spent his mornings breathing on his library window and playing noughts and crosses in the condensation, drinking gin as he did so.

In a letter to his daughter Margaret dated December 1965 Waugh wrote, 'The awful prospect is that I may have more than 20 years ahead . . . Don't let me in my dotage oppress you . . .' But he was not to live another 20 years. On Easter Sunday 1966, after he and his family had celebrated Mass at the nearby Catholic chapel, Evelyn Waugh suffered a sudden and fatal heart attack, releasing him from the ignominy of an empty and unsolicited old age.

Family man
(right) Though he often lost his temper, Waugh the family man was far from the Victorian ogre that he sometimes posed as. He was a loving father to his six children, and fiercely loyal to his wife. For her part, Laura Waugh always coped patiently with her husband's idiosyncrasies.

Mark Gerson/Weidenfeld Archive

'Stinkers'
(below) Piers Court, at Stinchcombe in Gloucestershire, was the Waugh family home for 18 years. Well-proportioned and elegant, the 18th-century manor house was a haven from the modern world, and Waugh did much of his work there.

Private Collection/Weidenfeld Archive

VILE BODIES

In what became one of the cult novels of its time, Waugh casts a cynical eye over the frantic, pleasure-seeking world of the Bright Young Things, and reveals himself a master of satire.

Vile Bodies is a devastatingly funny attack on the moral and cultural decay of society's élite between the world wars. Scene after scene of absurdly comic events unfolds through sharply spoken dialogue between a dazzling array of characters. The novel's fast and furious pace reflects the lifestyle of the people it satirizes, as the characters move from party to party in their quest for constant excitement.

The book was an immediate success, gaining a cult following among readers who mimicked the 'too thrill-making' language of the novel's Bright Young Things. As in all good satire, behind the comic façade lies a serious note. *Vile Bodies* seems to revel in the colourful decadence it parodies, but it gradually unveils the dreadful emptiness beneath the glitter.

GUIDE TO THE PLOT

The book opens with descriptions of a rough sea voyage from France to England in which most of the central characters are on board. The hero, Adam Fenwick-Symes, has just written his first novel and is returning to marry his fiancée Nina Blount. But his manuscript is impounded by customs officials and burnt, reversing his fortunes in one cruel blow. "Adam, angel, don't fuss or we shall miss the train," says Agatha Runcible, prominent

socialite and friend, impatient to reach London for a party.

The first part of that evening is spent in the parlour at Lottie Crump's hotel in Mayfair, with an assortment of people in varying states of drunkenness. Having lost his immediate prospects of marriage along with his manuscript, Adam is overjoyed when he wins £1000 on the flip of a coin. After a rushed phonecall to Nina to tell her the wedding is on again, he entrusts the money to a "drunk Major" who promises to put it on a horse and make Adam rich. Needless to say, the Major disappears, leaving Adam to call off the marriage again.

Further unlikely events are in store: as part of a die-hard group from Archie Schwert's party, Adam and Nina find themselves the guests of timid Miss Brown who offers whisky and breakfast in the small hours at her parents' home. Agatha Runcible stays overnight, still dressed in Hawaiian costume, and discovers to her embarrassment the next morning that Miss Brown's father is in fact the Prime Minister. Headlines of "Midnight orgies at No. 10" are enough to topple the Government.

Nina persuades Adam to ask her father for money so that they can marry. Nervous and hung over, Adam journeys to Doubting Hall and the eccentric Colonel Blount. At the end of a bizarre

day he departs deliriously happy, having obtained a cheque for £1000. What he does not notice, however, is that the Colonel has signed it 'Charlie Chaplin'.

Needing a regular income, Adam takes on the job of gossip columnist for a daily paper and when copy is short, he fabricates a collection of "Notable Invalids" and "Titled Eccentrics". Enjoying his influence, he goes on to invent a gallery of fashionable people and new unlikely styles of clothing. His job is short-lived, however, and once again his marriage to Nina is called off.

In search of more excitement, Adam and his friends drive up to the motor races – an outing that proves disastrous from the beginning. The usual round of fun becomes a surreal nightmare with Agatha Runcible finding herself at the wheel of one of the cars. The drunk Major turns up owing Adam £35,000, only to borrow "a fiver" and disappear again. The town is bursting with spectators, making it impossible to find a room for the night or even anywhere to eat. Dispirited and much the worse for wear, the group learns that Agatha has driven off the track and crashed the racing car.

The novel has begun its sudden rush forward to inevitable catastrophe. "How people are *disappearing*," laments Miss Runcible from her nursing home. Nina forsakes Adam and marries Ginger, a bore with money. But she and Adam are

Drunken nights
Basking in the cluttered elegance of Lottie Crump's parlour (right), the ex-King of Ruritania mourns his fate to anyone who will listen. And with champagne flowing like water, our unlucky hero Adam wins and loses £1000 in an evening of mixed fortunes.

Mary Evans Picture Library

Rough passage

A writer, a Jesuit and an MP are just a few of the cast of characters who confront sea-sickness and customs officials as they make their dramatic return to Britain's shores.

KENNETH D SHOESMITH

briefly united at her father's house for Christmas while Ginger is conscripted to serve in the war which is about to be declared. Colonel Blount, more confused and demented than ever, insists on showing *The Life of John Wesley*, the ridiculous film produced at his home, into which he has sunk all his fortune. The book concludes with the chapter entitled "Happy Ending", which depicts the bleak devastation of the battle-field where the remaining characters wander – lost, seeking solace in wine, debauchery and the oblivion of sleep.

SOCIAL SATIRE

Vile Bodies satirizes a particular social class in a particular era, but it contains a share of human truth, which gives the novel a lasting quality. With comic genius, Waugh ridicules the desolate world of casual injustice and betrayal, exposing the ineptitude and corruption endemic in a society preoccupied with sensual gratification.

The fantastical train of events trips and tumbles through to its ill-fated conclusion, enabling Waugh to level his

Lucien Adrion: A Day at the Races/Newman & Cooling/Fine Art Photographic Library

Winning and losing

Sent to cover the November Handicap for the Daily Excess, *Adam sees his horse, Indian Runner, come an easy first. But the drunk Major to whom he has given £1000 to put on the horse disappears into the crowd . . .*

Daring decadence

The endless succession of parties breeds a spirit of 'anything goes'. "Almost naked parties in St John's Wood" are just one of the entertainments.

"'Who's that awful-looking woman? I'm sure she's famous in some way. It's not Mrs Melrose Ape, is it? I heard she was coming.'
'Who?'
'That one. Making up to Nina.'
'Good lord, no. She's no one. Mrs Panrast she's called now.'
'She seems to know you.'
'Yes, I've known her all my life. As a matter of fact, she's my mother.'
'My dear, how too shaming.'"

The older generation
While the Young Set frolic from party to party, their elders cluck disparagingly about the state of the world.

attack far more effectively than if he were writing in a realistic mode. His weapons are wit, irony and parody which conspire to reveal a gross materialism containing the seeds of its own destruction. No-one is spared Waugh's sharp ridicule: greedy publishers, imbecilic politicians, shallow socialites, dissembling media people and purveyors of religion.

Walter Outrage, the muddle-headed Prime Minister, is portrayed as utterly unfit for office. The last to know anything about the war looming near, he complains: "No one has said anything to me about a war. I really think I should have been told. I'll be damned . . . What do they want a war for anyway?"

Mrs Melrose Ape, the "extremely dangerous and disagreeable" evangelist with her troupe of 'angels' named after forgotten human virtues, comes in for similar treatment. Modelled on the

American crusader Aimee Semple McPherson, she treats religion as a money-spinner, bullying her audiences into emotional confessions before swooping in for the kill. "'Salvation doesn't do them any good if they think it's free' was her favourite axiom." Portrayed as a perversion of godliness, she is hugely conceited, in many respects more a procurer than a preacher: "Hope's what you want and Hope's what I got," she announces firmly to an assembled group, while some of her more discontented 'angels' plot their escape to more lucrative employment. The ironically named 'Chastity' goes on to join a dance troupe in South America. She finally ends up as a much abused military plaything on both sides of the enemy lines, in England and abroad.

Lawson Wood: A Warm Corner/Felix Rosenstiel's Widow & Son/Bridgeman Art Library

Mary Evans Picture Library

In the Background

GOSSIP COLUMNS

Following World War I, gossip columns became a feature of many of the daily papers. Lord Northcliffe advised his journalists on the *Daily Mail* to 'Get more names in the paper – the more aristocratic the better.' Members of the upper classes were enticed into becoming gossip writers; they made enemies of their friends but were courted as royalty by such people as restaurant and golf-club managers. And for this they earned vast salaries – infinitely more than their senior editors.

A chatterbox's fate
A gossip columnist had to keep his titillating copy within acceptable social bounds – or lose his material and his job. In Vile Bodies, Simon Balcairn offends the society hostess Margot Metroland, and is barred from her party. He attempts to infiltrate it without success – and then resorts to desperate measures . .

John Frost Historical Newspaper Service

> *"I don't think people ever want to lose their faith either in religion or anything else. I know very few young people, but it seems to me that they are all possessed with an almost fatal hunger for permanence. I think all these divorces show that. People aren't content just to muddle along nowadays . . ."*

In the opening chapter, the diverse collection of passengers on the boat, in order "to avert the terrors of sea-sickness", are described as having "indulged in every kind of civilised witch-craft, but they were lacking in faith." At the heart of *Vile Bodies* lies this central concern of Waugh's: a world without faith is by definition a world without compassion, fidelity and stability. No-one will ever find lasting happiness and satisfaction in a godless universe. Instead, the characters in *Vile Bodies* entrust themselves to fortune and never know from one moment to the next what the future holds for them.

Agatha Runcible whirls from party to party becoming more selfishly careless at each turn. At the motor races, 'beneficent Providence' saves her when she throws a lighted cigarette in the direction of an open petrol drum, but nothing can save her when she takes over the wheel of car number 13. In a drunken state she drives off, soon leaving the track and crashing miles away from any recognizable location. She is found wandering around Euston Station the next morning explaining "that to the best of her knowledge she had no name . . . she had come in a motor car . . . which would not stop . . . There had been a stone thing in the way. They shouldn't put up symbols like that in the middle of the road, should they, or should they?" Ironically enough, "the stone thing" was a market cross . . . Miss Runcible's days as a symbol of all that is brightest and most outrageously divine in the Younger Set are over.

Our hero Adam, while following the same reckless existence, is more perceptive than his peers and knows that he wants something more. Just as he has an aromatic fantasy early one morning that "No kipper is ever as good as it smells . . . ", he knows that the anticipation of earthly pleasure is far more rewarding than the thing itself. Tired of the parties and "all that succession and repetition of massed humanity . . . Those vile bodies . . ." he asks, "Nina, do you ever feel that things simply can't go on much longer?" and later says wistfully "I'd give anything in the world for something different."

SPIRITUAL BANKRUPTCY

Bankrupt spiritually as well as financially, Adam is unlikely to get help from any of the other characters in the novel. Anyone who has anything to do with religion is as "*bogus*" as the film about John Wesley. Even the Jesuit Father Rothschild stands as a target for Waugh's satire. Described as "a charlatan", he carries a false beard in a borrowed suitcase of imitation crocodile and loves nothing more than to generate political intrigue.

Nevertheless it is Father Rothschild who takes Waugh's own voice at one point, saying without tongue in cheek, "Wars don't start nowadays because people want them. We long for peace, and fill our newspapers with conferences about disarmament and arbitration, but there is a radical instability in our whole world-order . . . " And it is certainly not by coincidence that the one character who is allowed to comment directly on the degenerate state of the world is a member, like Waugh, of the Roman Catholic Church.

The motor races
(left) Grabbing the wheel of no. 13, Agatha completes the course in record time . . .

Final devastation
(below) The characters seek what solace they can, against a war-scarred landscape.

CHARACTERS IN FOCUS

The characters in *Vile Bodies* are comic distortions of particular types. At times verging on caricature, they are central to the novel, and are the means by which Waugh launches his attack on the values and lifestyle of the upper classes. With the exception of Adam Fenwick-Symes, there is little to endear us to any of these people apart from their outrageous, inadvertent humour. We may not like the Mrs Melrose Apes of the world but we are unlikely to forget them.

WHO'S WHO

Adam Fenwick-Symes Looking "exactly as young men like him do look", he remains ever-hopeful of getting married.

Nina Blount Languid and easily bored, she is Adam's sometime fiancée and lover.

Colonel Blount Nina's father. An enthusiastic, eccentric old man, with a delightfully odd sense of humour.

Agatha Runcible Ever 'thrill-seeking', she is dependably outrageous.

Father Rothschild The all-knowing Jesuit priest who makes it his business to mix with people of influence.

Mrs Melrose Ape "An extremely dangerous and disagreeable woman", she promises salvation – for a price.

Lottie Crump Ageing proprietress of Shepheard's Hotel, she provides the good things of life for her favoured clientèle.

Ginger Littlejohn Foolish but blessed with money, he reappears after years of "doing something military" in Ceylon.

Archie Schwert A social climber, "rather sweet, really, only too terribly common".

The Drunk Major "A stout, red-faced man" who repeatedly fails to deliver Adam's £35,000.

Walter Outrage MP Unaware that a war is looming, the former Prime Minister is as unsuccessful a politician as he is a lover.

Given to occasional 'pains', Nina Blount (below) is the eccentric Colonel Blount's daughter and Adam Fenwick-Symes' sweetheart. Young and pretty, she epitomizes the boredom and emptiness of their world, going from one party to the next, when pains permit, but with no particular purpose. Adam's "poor, sweet Angel", she is sympathetic if somewhat spineless – "a girl who likes nice clothes and things . . . comfort and all that", and knows how to get them. Although she is fond of Adam, she is ultimately fonder of her comforts, and so throws him over for another. But with a self-indulgence characteristic of all the Bright Young Things, she does not let a minor detail like a marriage stand in the way of her happiness; and the War is not without its compensations . . .

Mild-mannered and innocent, Adam (below) is the most likable of the cast of characters. Unlike the other Bright Young Things he would "give anything in the world for something different", but events overtake him. His precious manuscript is destroyed; his publisher cancels his fee; he gets an unexpected windfall which then disappears in the hands of a drunk Major; and a cheque for £1000 also proves a red herring. Finally his fiancée, Nina, decides to leave him. But all is not calamity – Adam writes an extremely popular gossip column for a time, has moments of "jigging to himself in simple high spirits", buys his way out of Lottie Crump's bad books with amazing presence of mind, and actually does 'get' his girl – if not forever, at least once in a while . . .

Julian Puckett

"Not a tart", but "poor Viola Chasm's daughter", Agatha Runcible (right) is the most flamboyantly eccentric of the Bright Young Things. Changing her outfit at the drop of a hat, she is an alleged jewel smuggler, "a sort of dancing Hottentot woman half-naked", a hermaphrodite in men's trousers and a record-breaking racing car driver. "The life and soul of the evening", Agatha is popular among her own set as the symbol of wild youth. But with her, the spirit of 'anything goes' is taken to the point of madness. She seems hell-bent on a course of self-destruction, and no-one is there to stop her. Even after her car crash, recovering in an exclusive nursing home in Wimpole Street, she is ready for a party. With a gramophone under the bed, she directs Adam to the "cocktail things in the wardrobe". "Do make a big one", she urges, "the nurses love them so".

"A fine figure of a woman", Lottie Crump (above) is "a happy reminder to us that the splendours of the Edwardian era were not entirely confined to Lady Anchorage or Mrs Blackwater." Famed proprietress of Shepheard's Hotel, Dover Street, she is "singularly unscathed by any sort of misfortune and superbly oblivious to those changes in the social order which agitate the more observant *grandes dames* of her period". Hostess to the rich and famous, she gladly extends her patronage to aristocratic youths and deposed kings.

Possessing a keen eye and acute intelligence, Father Rothschild (right) is to be found scheming among the rich and powerful – "few of them were unknown to the Jesuit, for it was his happy knack to remember everything that could possibly be learned about everyone . . . of any importance." Although an absurd figure, his assessment of "the radical instability of our whole world order" is not far wrong.

SAVAGE HUMOUR

Comedy, farce and a streak of pessimism characterize Waugh's writing. His vivid sense of life's absurdities won over his readers, despite the scathing quality of his wit.

On 21 February 1927, after being sacked from his job as a schoolmaster, Evelyn Waugh confided to his diary that 'It seems to me the time has arrived to set about being a man of letters.' And this is exactly what he did. Within a few weeks he had begun to write a biography of the Victorian poet and painter Dante Gabriel Rossetti, and by the end of the year work on his first novel, *Decline and Fall*, was well advanced.

Both books were published in 1928, and from then onwards Waugh earned his living exclusively by his pen. After the popular success of *Vile Bodies* (1930), the living should have been a comfortable one. But thanks to his expensive social life, Waugh was generally short of money and willing to tackle more ephemeral work. At one point early in his career he was so desperate that he told his agent he was prepared to take on anything, 'even cricket criticism or mothers' welfare notes'.

As a result, Waugh published quantities of journalism over the years, ranging from 'The Mothers of the Younger Generation' to highly serious literary and religious writings. Incidentally, the aforementioned 'Mothers of the Younger Generation' came about through a comic misinterpretation worthy of one of Waugh's novels: he had proposed writing an article on 'The *Manners* of the Younger Generation', but an editor misread his bad handwriting – and commissioned 'Mothers', which Waugh proceeded to turn out in true professional style.

Travel gave Waugh another welcome source of income, as well as providing him with an outlet for the restlessness of his middle years. Apart from journalistic dispatches from abroad, he also wrote six travel books, collecting what he considered to be the best parts in a single volume, *When the Going Was Good* (1946). His experience of Africa (mainly Ethiopia) was particularly valuable; it is the setting for no less than four of his books, including the satirical novels *Black Mischief* (1932) and *Scoop* (1938). Waugh's contemptuous opinion of journalism and journalists finds its most hilarious expression in *Scoop*.

Waugh's opinions, sharply expressed, also appear in the diaries and letters he wrote (both published since his death), and in his account of his early life, *A Little Learning* (1964). Although at first mistaken by many people for a celebrator of the amoral Bright Young Things of the 1920s and '30s, he was always in reality a traditionalist, increasingly dismayed by the 20th century.

His comic genius took full advantage of the absurdities Waugh observed, but his personal feelings were expressed by his classics-master hero in the long story *Scott-King's Modern Europe* (1947). Invited to teach a more 'relevant' subject than classics, Mr Scott-King answers

THE HEADMASTER'S HOUSE
requests the honour of your company
on Sunday, June 19th. at 7·45 p.m. in
the Great School at a performance of

CONVERSION

the tragedy of Youth in three burlesques,
by
EVELYN WAUGH.

Act I.   School, as maiden Aunts think it is.
Act II. School, as modern authors say it is
Act III. School, as we all know it is.

R.S.V.P.   F.E.Ford.

Early promise
(above) Waugh's first play, written while he was a pupil at Lancing College in Sussex, was a satire on public-school life.

Writer or artist?
At Oxford, Waugh was as inclined to drawing as he was to writing. He designed the cover of Harold Acton's magazine, Oxford Broom (right) and contributed articles and drawings to numerous other periodicals.

novels he published after World War II. On finishing *Brideshead Revisited* (1945), Waugh considered it his masterpiece, 'full of literary power' in its description of 'the operation of divine grace on a group of diverse but closely connected characters'. The public agreed, buying 600,000 copies and putting Waugh – somewhat to his embarrassment – into the best-seller class.

By contrast with his earlier work, *Brideshead* was written in a lusher style that Waugh came to regret, and which he blamed on the fact that it was composed 'at a very bad time in the war when there was nothing to eat . . . The fact that it is rich in evocative description – in gluttonous writing – is the direct result of the privations of the times.' For many readers, however, the sumptuous lifestyle and aristocratic splendours of Oxford and Brideshead are the very heart of the novel.

World War II is more overtly the

D. G. Rossetti: La Ghirlandata/Guildhall Art Gallery/Bridgeman Art Library

Surface glitter
(left) At first glance, Waugh seems to celebrate the frivolous lifestyle of the Smart Set – but he was a man of strong moral views who used his pen to expose the emptiness beneath the glitter.

austerely, "I think it would be very wicked indeed to do anything to fit a boy for the modern world." Surprisingly, Waugh's ardent Roman Catholic faith provided only limited consolation, although it did give his serious novels a much-needed positive element.

CONCENTRATED SATIRE

Readers are often inclined to disagree strongly about the relative merits of Waugh's novels. Many believe that he was at his best as a satirist, writing short, dazzlingly concentrated tales in which not a word is wasted and event is piled upon event in an exhilarating brew of comedy and farce. In the satires, the reader is carried along, accepting all of Waugh's prejudices and partialities, into a hard-edged world where love and loyalty are at a discount and even the innocent heroes and victims have no inkling of moral sense. *Decline and Fall*, *Vile Bodies*, *A Handful of Dust* (1934) and *The Loved One* (1948) have all been nominated at various times as Waugh's best work.

Other readers prefer the ambitious

Rossetti
(above right) The work of the Pre-Raphaelite painter, Dante Gabriel Rossetti, was the subject of Waugh's first major publication. To his fury, one critic referred to him as 'Miss Waugh'!

A runaway success
(right) Waugh designed this frontispiece for the first edition of Vile Bodies *in 1930. It was this novel's success that confirmed Waugh's reputation. 'I laughed till I was driven out of the room', was the reaction of one reviewer.*

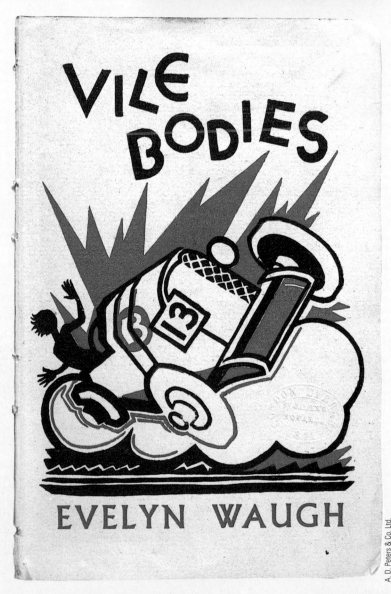

A. D. Peters & Co. Ltd.

War correspondent
(left) Waugh covered the Italian invasion of Abyssinia in 1935 for the Daily Mail. He fell out with his editors after missing a scoop, and was finally dismissed – but the war gave him a rich source of material for his fiction.

Craftsman
(below) In his 'workshop', surrounded by his books and precious mementoes, Waugh meticulously revised his novels.

subject of Waugh's final large-scale work of fiction, the *Sword of Honour* trilogy (1965). A famous historian, A. J. P. Taylor, says simply that 'Now, if future generations want to know what the Second World War was like, they can safely be referred to the trilogy by Evelyn Waugh.' The hero, Guy Crouchback, has sometimes been dismissed as too negative a being, though Waugh called him 'essentially an unselfish character', and when the moment comes he seizes the chance of salvation by making himself responsible for another man's child. In scale and ambition, at least, *Sword of Honour* surpasses all of Waugh's other works.

Nevertheless, Evelyn Waugh's fictional world has distinct limits. All his important characters are taken from the upper and upper-middle classes, since theirs was the world he knew best, and was the only one that interested him. Waugh never tried to create a social panorama, or even to explore character in depth. As he told an interviewer, 'I regard writing not as an investigation of character, but as an exercise in the use of language, and with this I am obsessed . . . It is drama, speech, and events that interest me . . . You see, there are always words going round in my head; some people think in pictures, some in ideas. I think entirely in words. By the time I come to stick my pen in my ink pot these words have reached a stage of order which is fairly presentable.'

A NATURAL NOVELIST

This is very much a craftsman's view of writing, emphasizing the ordering of the thing produced rather than the psychology of the producer. Waugh, like his alter ego Gilbert Pinfold, "regarded his books as objects which he had made, things quite external to himself to be used and judged by others". This meant that he could dismiss questions about his own life as irrelevant and impertinent, and that he could object violently when people tried to identify the real-life originals of his characters, despite the fact that some of these were unmistakable.

Furthermore, Waugh revealed very little about his working methods, or about the way in which his novels evolved. Yet, it is clear that he was a natural novelist – he composed his first work of fiction when he was seven and, by his own account, took no more than six weeks over each of his early novels. And although he jealously guarded the secrets of his workshop, his books inevitably constitute an unintended portrait of Evelyn Waugh's difficult, troubled personality.

WORKS·IN OUTLINE

With his great gift for comedy, Evelyn Waugh was the outstanding satirist of the 1930s, before staking his claims as a serious novelist. *Decline and Fall* (1928) introduced the world of Bright Young Things, and its successor, *Vile Bodies* (1930), brought Waugh fame and money.

Black Mischief (1932) and *Scoop* (1938) drew heavily on his experiences in Africa. In *Put Out More Flags* (1942) characters from the earlier novels adapt themselves to wartime. Waugh wrote only one more satire, *The Loved One* (1948). *Brideshead Revisited* (1945) evokes the glamour of aristocratic life before the war, and reveals Waugh's religious concerns, also evident in his non-fiction. *Men at Arms* (1952) and *Officers and Gent-*lemen (1955), both about World War II, follow the fortunes of Guy Crouchback. *The Ordeal of Gilbert Pinfold* (1957) is a thinly disguised account of Waugh's mental breakdown.

Waugh completed his war trilogy (known as *Sword of Honour*) with *Unconditional Surrender* (1961); before his death in 1966 he finished one volume of autobiography, *A Little Learning* (1964).

DECLINE AND FALL
◆ 1928 ◆

Decadent 'fallen women' (right) feature in Paul Pennyfeather's rites of passage. This unworldly hero, sent down from his Oxford college for 'indecent behaviour' after being 'de-bagged', becomes a schoolmaster at the awful Llanabba Castle (below), where one of his colleagues is the disreputable Captain Grimes. Paul falls in love with Margot Beste-Chetwynde, the mother of a pupil, who whisks him away from Llanabba and introduces him into high society. They are about to be married when Paul is arrested and, taking the blame for Margot, convicted of being a white slave trader. He receives a seven-year prison sentence and is sent to Egdon Heath gaol. Margot – now married to the influential Lord Metroland – engineers Paul's release, and, one year after losing his trousers, he finds himself, literally, back where he started from.

C. R. W. Nevinson: Amongst the Nerves of the World, 1930/Museum of London

SCOOP
◆ 1938 ◆

Unscrupulous Fleet Street (left) is satirized in this story where a newspaper proprietor sends the wrong correspondent to cover a foreign war. Lord Copper, owner of *The Daily Beast*, means to send fashionable novelist John Boot. But William Boot, a rustic innocent who writes nature notes for the *Beast*, is given the assignment instead. In the Ishmaelian capital of Jacksonburg, Boot is introduced to the colourful ways of foreign reporting and falls in love with a German girl. Not wanting to leave her, he stays behind when fellow journalists rush off to a non-existent trouble spot – and as a result scoops the world when a Marxist coup is staged in the capital. His dispatches home earn him overnight fame and on his return to England he is due to be fêted and to receive a knighthood – but once more, plans go awry . . .

Otto Dix': Urban Debauchery/Galerie der Stadt, Stuttgart/Fabbri/Bridgeman Art Library

BRIDESHEAD REVISITED

←1945→

Beautiful memories of university days (left), come flooding back for Charles Ryder when he is stationed at Brideshead Castle, the palatial country house of the Marchmain family during World War II. The main narrative begins as Charles recalls his student friendship with the wilful, eccentric Sebastian Flyte, younger son of the Marquis of Marchmain. Through Sebastian he visits Brideshead and meets the devoutly Catholic Lady Marchmain, and her daughter Julia. Lord Marchmain, denied a divorce, lives abroad with his mistress.

Despite the efforts of Ryder and of his own family, Sebastian sinks into alcoholism and eventually disappears to North Africa.

Charles Ryder's involvement with the family continues. Now a successful artist, he falls in love with Julia; both are unhappily married, and they decide to make a new start together. But their plans are disturbed when Lady Marchmain dies and her erring husband comes back to Brideshead. On his deathbed Lord Marchmain returns to Roman Catholicism – a decision that has the profoundest consequences for the lovers.

THE LOVED ONE

←1948→

A young English poet's experience of bizarre funeral practices (right) among wealthy Californians is the focus of this caustic view of post-war America. Dennis Barlow comes to the end of his contract as a Hollywood scriptwriter and – to the horror of the expatriate community – takes a job in a pets' cemetery. But the ceremonious absurdities of the Happier Hunting Ground pale in comparison with the expensively 'artistic' arrangements at nearby Whispering Glades, a 'Memorial Park' for humans. Here, all is life and beauty – even "the Loved One", or corpse, is glowingly preserved, thanks to the ministrations of the senior mortician, Mr Joyboy, and his admiring assistants. These include the beautiful but vacuous Aimée Thanatogenous, who is wooed by both Mr Joyboy and Dennis, the latter eager to conceal the fact that he is a humble employee in the same line of business. Dennis wins her heart with his love poems, all of them copied out from the *Oxford Book of English Verse,* but eventually his impostures are exposed, Aimée turns to Mr Joyboy, and everything appears to be settled. Then, suddenly, the plot takes a tragic turn, for Aimée becomes in all senses of the word the Loved One . . .

THE LOVED ONE
An Anglo-American Tragedy
by
EVELYN WAUGH
Illustrated by
STUART BOYLE

Chapman & Hall

THE ORDEAL OF GILBERT PINFOLD

◆ 1957 ◆

Crusty recluse Gilbert Pinfold goes briefly mad in this most directly autobiographical of all Waugh's novels. Like Waugh (left), Pinfold is a middle-aged writer of some distinction who dislikes the modern world, offering it "a front of pomposity mitigated by indiscretion, that was as hard, bright and antiquated as a cuirass". He drinks too much and takes dangerously liberal doses of chloral and bromide in crème-de-menthe as a sleeping draught. When he begins to suffer strange lapses of memory, Pinfold decides to get away into the sun, and at short notice manages to book a passage on the *Caliban,* a passenger ship bound for Ceylon. From the beginning of the voyage he 'overhears' bizarre incidents that take place among the crew, and extraordinarily offensive remarks made by his fellow passengers. Then he is persecuted by the verbal abuse of Angel and Goneril, while Angel's sister Margaret subjects him to declarations of girlish passion. A mysterious electrical device keeps him in constant contact with his unseen tormentors. On his return to London his wife helps him understand that most of the voices he has heard have been delusions and he prepares to write a book about it. He calls the book *The Ordeal of Gilbert Pinfold*.

SWORD OF HONOUR

◆ 1965 ◆

Experience of wartime (right) is the subject of this famous trilogy, which follows the fortunes of Guy Crouchback, an honourable, rather dull man who is deeply scarred by the failure of his marriage and finds little solace in his Catholic faith. Like many others, he believes that the war will give his life a meaning – the novels chart the progress of his disillusionment. In *Men at Arms* (1952) he joins the Royal Corps of Halberdiers and encounters the African veteran Apthorpe, who takes his 'thunderbox' (portable lavatory) with him everywhere, and the ferocious, one-eyed brigadier Ben Ritchie-Hook. In *Officers and Gentlemen* (1955) Guy transfers to the Commandos. The worthless ex-hairdresser Trimmer seduces Guy's shallow, silly ex-wife Virginia and despite his cowardice becomes a media-made national hero, while Guy is caught up in the British withdrawal from Crete and escapes to North Africa in an open boat. Back in London in *Unconditional Surrender* (1961) he remarries Virginia despite the fact that she is pregnant by Trimmer – this is Guy's gesture of charity in an increasingly corrupt world. He then serves in Yugoslavia, where the British are supporting a Communist takeover. Virginia is killed in the Blitz, leaving Guy a son and heir. Nevertheless, in time Guy achieves self-knowledge and finds in the post-war world an unexpected fullness of life.

THE ROARING TWENTIES

Following the horrors of the war years, music, razzmatazz and glitter were the order of the day. People partied into the small hours – and loved every minute of it.

The World War of 1914–18 was a cataclysmic event, which changed the world and people's perceptions to such an extent that a grown person looking back at 1913 from the vantage point of 1923 might as easily have been bridging a century as a decade. Today, it is difficult to identify with the world before 1914. The world of *Vile Bodies*, by contrast, seems somehow familiar. In practically every important respect it is the modern world, our world.

Of all the images of the Roaring Twenties, the most striking is that of a pert young woman – free, fun and gamely determined to tackle life as an independent human being. The Sixties Chelsea Girl in London had a lot in common with her 'flapper'

grandmother. If they were of a mind to do so they both held down a job, took an active interest in politics and viewed their parents as outdated 'fuddy-duddies'. Each lived for the moment and sought pleasure where they could. Slaves to transient fashion, the flappers and the Sixties children changed their attitudes as often as their dress, and seemed to court the disapproval of their elders. If they fancied it, each smoked and drank and maybe even dabbled in drugs with their men friends, and if they wanted to sleep with them they did that too. For both, the term 'Victorian' conveyed their disdain for boring, middle-aged attitudes.

NO TURNING BACK

The 'new woman', as she was described, was a direct product of the First World War. The war had opened up an enormous range of employment opportunities for women, and when it came to an end it was unthinkable that these new working women would all tamely retreat to hearth and home. At the same time, their contribution to the war effort was recognized by all, and in rapid succession a host of male bastions came tumbling down. Women were given the vote and allowed to stand for Parliament. An Act of Parliament in 1918 swept away barriers to most professions, including the Bar, while Cambridge followed Oxford's lead in opening the door to women fellows.

Young women from the middle and upper classes gained the most immediate and direct benefit from these changes, but the effects were felt throughout society. A working-class girl whose mother had spent her life in domestic service could see the wider horizons offered by secretarial work or a job behind the counter of a bustling department store.

Employment of this sort scarcely provided her with affluence, but it took her light years away from the world of 'Upstairs Downstairs'. She

The Jazz Age
After the war, couples boogied as never before. Everything had changed – the Charleston (right) was all the vogue, and black bands (left) could earn more in a single season than the British Prime Minister earned in a year.

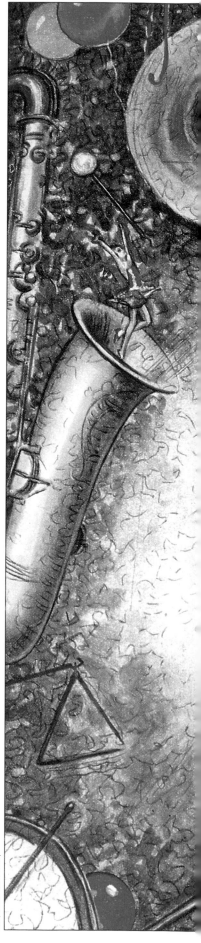

could move away from home and perhaps share a flat with other girls. She could go to the cinema, buy gramophone records and keep abreast of the latest dance craze. Also, being able to afford cheap make-up and inexpensive versions of the latest fashions meant that she was able to identify with a particular age group rather than just a particular class. The secretary sharing lodgings in a drab suburb was a member of the Younger Generation, just as Waugh's 'Bright Young Things' were.

This Younger Generation was bent on having a good time. The slaughter and sacrifice of the war had created almost universal disillusionment. At a philosophical level, this led to a withering assault on the comfortable assumptions of the Victorian Age, in particular on the belief that human beings were rational creatures able to control their own destiny. At an everyday level, this attitude bred cynicism and found expression in a craving for pleasure. Life is short, so make it sweet.

Reckless, defiant gaiety was the hallmark of the Roaring Twenties, and the Bright Young Things led the way. Waugh's bitchy little sketch of the privileged Mayfair set is hilariously funny, but it is right on target: the compulsive flitting from party to party in order to 'be with the action', as a later generation would put it; the wild, boisterous drinking; the infectious sense of irresponsibility; above all the obsession with having fun *all* the time (which was 'just too, *too* divine', as opposed to

Looking to the future
The 'new woman' left behind the trimmings of a former era, happy to display her femininity without props or buttresses. Hair was disarmingly short – like a man's – a symbol of woman's new-found independence and equality.

73

"That frock's so short you can
see your garters."

"Well well, my dear – I'll wear
them higher up!"

Changing fashions

*In the twenties, to show
the knee was considered
very daring, but the girl
(left) is clearly
unrepentant. Rather than
lengthen her skirt she
decides to tackle the
problem from the other
angle – raising her garters.
And to compound her sins
she has cropped hair,
defiantly bare arms and a
jauntily held cigarette.*

the small hours, and most night-club owners – and
their patrons – were quite prepared to flout the
law. Mrs. Kate Meyrick opened the first of her
clubs, the notorious '43' in Gerrard St, in 1921 and
went on to become the queen of London's night-
life. She cheerfully endured raids and fines until in
1924 she was sentenced to – and served – six months
in Holloway prison. This 'martyrdom' solidified
her social standing, and her three daughters
married into the aristocracy.

The private party had nothing to fear from any
licensing laws, and at times it appeared as though
the Bright Young Things were enjoying a non-stop
party, cavorting between their Mayfair heartland
and those distant outposts of Knightsbridge and
Chelsea. Their most publicized fling was the
'Babies' Ball', where they all rolled up in prams
and got wildly drunk prancing around in rompers
and pinafores. The innocent sounding Oxford
Railway Club was another symptom of this almost
calculated high-spiritedness. It was formed to extol
the pleasures of drinking through the night on

anything else, which was 'just too, *too* boring').

The fun began with the music – jazz imported
from the progressive and less inhibited United
States. With jazz came the new dances – the 'Camel
Walk', the 'Shimmy', and then the two really
outstanding dance crazes of the decade, the
'Charleston' and the 'Black Bottom'. The music
was lively, with pulsing, insistent rhythms and the
dance steps caught the energy of the music. Swank
hotels hastened to lay out dance floors, while an
easing of the strict wartime licensing hours gave
birth to a flourishing restaurant and cabaret scene.
Drinking as such was curbed at 11 pm, but it was
easy to get around that by ordering a sandwich,
which extended the period to 12.30 am.

PARTIES AND NIGHT-CLUBS

Another tremendously successful American
import was the cocktail, and with it came the
cocktail party. The gin-based cocktail encountered
stern resistance amongst the older generation, not
so much because of its American origin but because
of the Victorian association of gin with lower-class
drunkenness. The cocktail party too – a brief, early-
evening whirl of chattering – seemed odd to those
who remembered leisurely Edwardian house
parties. Why were the young in so much of a hurry?

Night-clubs dotted London's West End. Some
of them were highly respectable and obeyed the
law by serving drinks only up to the appointed
hour. But essentially night-clubs existed to provide
revellers with the chance to enjoy themselves into

Sports and pleasure

*As women divested
themselves of cumbersome
clothes, they were able to
compete more equally
with men in the field of
sports. Money helped
too, and the fashionable
set had time to kill on
Europe's tennis courts
and golf courses (above).
But swimming pools
could provide more
elaborate entertainment.
Fancy-dress parties were
in vogue and people went
to extraordinary lengths
to outdo their friends.
Entire baths would be
rented for swimming
parties and guests could
come in colour-coordinated
outfits or bearing their
own white horse (right).*

trains, and its members, who included Evelyn Waugh, would board the Penzance-Aberdeen express at Oxford, attired in full evening dress. They would proceed to drink their way to Leicester, disembark, and catch the southbound train – roistering all the way back to Oxford and the cold light of dawn.

Such innovative and exorbitant ways of getting drunk touched the lives of the pampered few, but there were cheaper crazes which were open to all. Anyone, for instance, could hop about on a Pogo Stick, and in the autumn of 1921 just about everyone did. This curious contraption – a spring-loaded pole with cross-bars for hands and feet – has ever since held a passing attraction for children, but it is hard to imagine grown men and women bouncing along the pavement. It was simply a fad – one more transient phase – as were so many Twenties' pastimes. The Chinese game Mah-Jong was all the rage by mid-decade, and so was the American-imported crossword puzzle.

OUTRAGEOUS EXCESS

Such fads, along with the comings and goings of the fashionable set, were staple fare for the gossip columns of society magazines and popular newspapers. But side by side with the journalistic sensationalism and titillation which features in *Vile Bodies* came a heartfelt condemnation of youthful frivolity. The war had given young people

Broders: Vichy Comité des Fêtes France. 1920 © DACS 1989/Paul Bremen Collection, USA/Bridgeman Art Library

Extravagant pleasures
Even the wealthy had felt the pinch of the war years. When it was over they treated themselves to lavish distractions.

unprecedented respect in the eyes of their elders, but that did not give them *carte blanche* to dress and behave wildly.

There was much fulminating about women's fashions. Women in factories during the war had found it safer and more convenient to cut their hair short and wear trousers. Bobbed hair, trousers and short skirts became badges of the flapper, along with facial make-up, another American import. And it was lamented that the very shape of young women had undergone a dramatic change for the worse in a single generation. Where had those pleasingly ample, fetchingly corsetted Edwardian figures gone? Could those skinny little things whose scanty clothing barely concealed a non-existent bust really be their daughters?

SLEEKER FIGURES

There were, in fact, good reasons for many of these changes. Severe shortages of sugar and butter during the war years had meant that the young had grown into the habit of doing with little. Having become accustomed to imposed slimming, it was then easy for them to slim for fashion. This change in diet was accompanied by other changes too. The enormous gulf between men and women had been narrowed – women could now work, vote, smoke, drive – so it seemed logical that they

75

T. C. Dugdale: Jarrow Marchers/Geffrye Museum, London

should be able to dress more boyishly too.

Flappers – so called because they sat on the 'flapper-bracket' riding pillion on motorcycles – were easy targets for satire. *Punch* published this biting parody in 1922:

> But whether you behold her in her box
> Diaphonously clad, with purple locks,
> Or jazzing with contortions that outdo
> The gestures of a boxing kangaroo . . .
> Glorinda holds the centre of the stage,
> The most conspicuous monster of our age.

Less trivial than concerns about fashion and frantic dancing was an underlying fear among many that women's new independence and the sexual freedom that everyone seemed to talk about would undermine the hierarchical edifice of family life. Women were at last given the vote on the same terms as men in 1928; Dr. Marie Stopes was making headway in her tireless campaign to spread information on birth control so that women could escape the dangerous burden of excessive pregnancies; divorces were becoming widespread, at least among those above the reach of middle-class morality. Society was changing.

And as the decade drew to a close, so too did the pleasure-obsessed world of *Vile Bodies*. The collapse of the American stock market, the Wall Street Crash of 1929, devastated the economy of the United States and had terrible repercussions in Britain. The glitter of the twenties was replaced by the Depression of the thirties. While the Depression hit the ordinary people (who had no place in Waugh's world) hardest, even for the likes of Adam and Nina, the party was over.

The Thirties

(below) The bubble of 1920s gaiety burst with the Depression of the following decade. Driven to action, a throng of unemployed workers from the shipyards and iron and steel works of the North marched on London in protest. Only a lucky few (left) were untouched by these struggles and could look on at the marchers with sublime indifference.

BBC Hulton Picture Library

ALDOUS HUXLEY

⟶1894-1963⟵

One of the outstanding intellectual figures of the 20th century,
Aldous Huxley was blessed with a mind capable of embracing
every field of human knowledge. A witty, acute social
commentator, he was hailed as the cynical spokesman of his
generation, yet retained a gentleness of character that won him
countless friends. He staked his literary reputation on advice
and warnings about human progress towards the future, eager
to maintain a balanced unity of Science, Nature and Humanity.

TENDER-HEARTED PESSIMIST

His prophetic visions seemed doom-laden, but Huxley was a gentle, compassionate man 'in whom wisdom never destroyed innocence'.

Aldous Huxley was not only one of the outstanding writers of his generation, illuminating every subject he touched with a remarkably original intelligence, but also a man whose warmth, humanity, wit and courage in adversity made him a joy and inspiration to a brilliant circle of friends and admirers. His fellow writer Raymond Mortimer said of him: 'Nobody else I know has combined so fine a brain, such encyclopaedic knowledge and so deep a response to all the arts with such sweetness of character.'

A DISTINGUISHED FAMILY

Aldous Leonard Huxley was born on 26 July 1894 at a house called Laleham, near Godalming in Surrey. Socially he belonged to the upper middle class, but in intellectual terms he was born into the aristocracy. His father was Leonard Huxley, a fine classical scholar who was a master at Charterhouse School and later became editor of the *Cornhill Magazine*. His mother was Julia Frances (née Arnold), an exceptional woman who was the driving force of the family. The granddaughter of Dr Thomas Arnold (headmaster of Rugby school and a great educational reformer) and niece of the poet and critic Matthew Arnold, she – like her husband – gained a first-class degree at Oxford University. After having four children – Julian (who became an eminent biologist and philosopher), Trevenen, Aldous and Margaret – she established a school for girls at Prior's Field in Surrey. Her sons competed for her love and attention, and Julian later recalled that Aldous loved her 'passionately'.

Aldous came of distinguished lineage on the paternal side, too, for his grandfather was the eminent biologist, Thomas Henry Huxley, a freethinker and champion of Darwinism who gave the word 'agnostic' to the English language. Like his brothers, Aldous was encouraged to read widely from an early age and explore knowledge and ideas. His parents were affectionate and caring, but there was a price to pay for his upbringing: he had to do exceptionally well academically ('Huxleys always get Firsts') and was expected to stifle 'unseemly' emotions. It was this rigidity – characteristic of the repressive formality of Victorian England – against which Aldous, along with many other writers and artists of his generation, reacted. His rebellion was fuelled by three major tragedies in the space of six years: the death of his mother; a chronic eye infection; and the suicide of his brother Trevenen.

The first disaster occurred in November 1908, when Aldous, aged 14, was in his first term at Eton. His mother had cancer and died after a short illness, aged 45. The family was grief-stricken, but Aldous – 'very sensitive and brooding' – suppressed his feelings, and after he returned to school at Eton he distinguished himself academically, particularly in biology. He determined to become a doctor, but his dreams suffered a shattering blow when, in 1911, he suddenly developed a serious infection in both eyes. Sent home from Eton, he

By kind permission of Matthew Huxley

Father and sons
Close-knit and gifted as they were, the Huxleys were dogged by tragedy. The suicide of Trevenen (above right) as a young man shattered his younger brother, Aldous (above).

Key Dates

1894 born in Surrey
1908 mother dies
1914 Trevenen dies
1919 marries Maria Nys
1932 *Brave New World*
1937 settles in the United States
1954 *The Doors of Perception*
1955 Maria dies
1956 marries Laura Archera
1962 elected a Companion of Literature
1963 dies in Los Angeles

Leigh Simpson: Eton College. Christopher Wood Gallery/Bridgeman Art Library

Thomas Huxley
*Over half a century before
Aldous became a student
at Balliol College (top),
his illustrious grandfather
(above) had shaken
Oxford's repose with his
vigorous and witty
support of Darwin's
theory of evolution.*

Eton College
*(left) Excelling at Eton,
like his brothers before
him, Aldous considered it
'a very good school'.*

suffered 18 months of virtual blindness, and his vision was strictly limited for the rest of his life.

Cut off from his friends, his ambitions in shreds, Aldous typically responded by doggedly learning Braille in order to continue his studies. When the infection subsided, he pored painfully over page after page with a huge magnifying glass; and with the help of various tutors, Aldous, like his brothers before him, became a student at Balliol College, Oxford.

Less than a year later, on 23rd August 1914, the 24-year-old Trevenen, who of all the family had done most to encourage his disabled younger brother, committed suicide. Comparatively poor Finals results and a hushed-up affair with the family's parlourmaid have been cited as the causes. For Aldous, however, the reason for Trevenen's death lay deeper. As he wrote to his cousin Gervas, 'It is the highest and best in Trev – his ideals – which have driven him to his death . . . Trev was not strong, but he had the courage to face life with ideals – and his ideals were too much for him.'

TRANSIENCE OF HAPPINESS

The cumulative force of these tragedies impressed upon Aldous a sense of the transience of happiness and the frailty of human life and a belief that high ideals alone were not enough to sustain a person. These impressions were reinforced as he watched many of his Oxford friends go blithely off to die for King and Country in the trenches of World War I. 'The West has plucked its flowers and has thrown/Them fading on the night', he wrote in *The Burning Wheel,* his first collection of poems, published in 1916.

Rejected by the army as totally unfit, he continued his studies, gaining a First in English in June 1916. He wrote triumphantly to his brother Julian: 'I should like to go on for ever learning. I lust for knowledge, as well theoretic and empirical.' The brilliant student cut an unusual figure: immensely tall (six feet four-and-a-half inches) with a pipecleaner frame, his almost sightless eyes emphasizing his charming, rather ethereal air of self-deprecation, he appeared the epitome of the underfed, overbred aesthete. Only his liking for floppy neckwear hinted at a streak of unconventional flamboyance.

After a short spell vainly attempting to do his bit for the war effort at the Air Board, Huxley gained a poorly paid teaching post at Eton. The holidays, however, he spent at Garsington Manor, the Oxfordshire home of Sir Philip and Lady Ottoline Morrell, providers of open house to the Bloomsbury Group of intellectuals, all of whom were opposed to the war. Huxley later recalled: 'The meeting of all these people was of capital importance to me.'

Garsington was a hothouse of culture, new ideas and permissiveness, unlike anything the withdrawn, fledgling writer had encountered before. While staying there in the summer of 1916, however, he met a soulmate in the 16-year-old Belgian refugee Maria Nys. Her innocence, spontaneity

The Writer's Life

Whitehall wanderings

In 1917, having failed his medical repeatedly because of poor eyesight, Huxley accepted a low-paid clerical job at the Air Board (right), wishing to do his bit for the war effort. But he was, understandably, entirely out of place there. Surrounded by people 'with absolutely no interest in life but making money and gossiping about their hideous homes', he ached from 'the soul-weariness with which this place overcomes one.'

R. Vicat Cole: Whitehall/Fine Art Photographic Library

and love of life he found irresistible. The pair fell in love and resolved to marry, but the war, Maria's youth and Aldous' lack of finances seemed insurmountable barriers. Finally after painful years of enforced separation, they were married in Belgium on 10 July 1919.

Maria, loyal, intuitive, loving and sociable, was to have a profound, healing effect on Aldous' life. For 36 years she nursed him through illness after illness, at all times doing everything she could to make his life as tranquil as possible. She was his 'eyes' and later his chauffeur on their countless tours of Europe and America; her sociability and charm brought him the human contact he craved and yet shrank from; she breathed vitality into the sterile, rarefied world of ideas that had threatened to become his prison.

The couple settled in a small flat in Hampstead, north-west London, Huxley having given up teaching and gained an editorial post at the *Athenaeum* magazine. In January 1920 *Limbo,* his first book of short stories, was published; in April, after an alarmingly difficult labour, Maria gave birth to their son Matthew. With a family to support, lack of money was a constant pressure, and Huxley took on extra work, becoming drama and music critic for the *Westminster Gazette,* and then working for *House & Garden.*

By the spring of 1921, they had saved enough to spend the summer in Italy, and it was there in Florence that Huxley completed his first novel, *Crome Yellow.* The critical success it received and also that of a subsequent volume of short stories, *Mortal Coils,* convinced publishers Chatto & Windus that Huxley was worth encouraging. In 1923 they offered him a contract which allowed him to

Ambrose McEvoy: Miss Nancy Cunard: Bradford City Art Gallery & Museums/Bridgeman Art Library

Nancy Cunard

An outrageous post-war socialite, the beautiful Nancy Cunard (above) was, briefly, the object of Huxley's sudden, passionate, unrequited love. Like one of his characters, he loved her "against reason, against all his ideals and principles, madly . . ."

devote himself from then on to his writing – a long-cherished dream.

Although £500 a year was not a large sum on which to live in London, it would keep his family in relative comfort in Italy, and in early summer of 1923 they moved there, settling in Florence in August. They left England under a cloud, for Huxley had become briefly and passionately involved with the unconventional Twenties socialite Nancy Cunard. The unhappy affair ended as suddenly as it had begun.

The voracious enthusiasm Aldous brought to intellectual pursuits now manifested itself in his desire to see the world. Over the next few years Aldous and Maria toured Italy, France, Holland and Belgium. In September 1925 they were bound for India. Huxley was singularly unimpressed at first by Hindu mysticism and India in general. 'India is depressing as no other country I have ever known. One breathes in it, not air, but dust and hopelessness', he wrote in his diary, published as *Jesting Pilate* in 1926. Interestingly, he was to change his mind profoundly about Indian culture later in life.

After a brief round-the-world trip, the Huxleys returned to England, then went back to Europe. In Florence they became close friends with the ailing

Fact or Fiction

GENETIC ENGINEERING

Huxley's alarming proph-ecy of a world shaped by genetic engineering might have come to pass had Hitler won World War II. The Nazi hierarchy was deeply inter-ested in 'improving' the Aryan race by selective, artifi-cial conception.

Some consider Huxley's vision has been realized – test-tube babies which were once the stuff of science fic-tion are now a scientific real-ity. But the author's warning that "in the context of nationalism, eugenics could become an instrument of extraordinary power and extraordinary danger" is still a nightmare possibility worth heeding.

Charlotte Raymond/Science Photo Library

Italian sojourns
Huxley and Maria first travelled to Florence (left) in April 1921. They were captivated, and often returned there, and to the surrounding countryside (below) over the years. Ideally, Huxley would have liked to spend half his time in Italy and half in England – the former for living, the latter for working, two pursuits which he felt he needed to do separately.

Antonietta Brandeis: The Pontevecchio, Florence. Savin Graham Gallery/Bridgeman Art Library

D. H. Lawrence and his wife Frieda. The couples continued to meet regularly up to Lawrence's death in 1930. Huxley enjoyed friendships with many famous artists and intellectuals, among them the great violinist Yehudi Menuhin and the art historian Kenneth Clark. Menuhin once said of Huxley, 'his voice was the gentlest melody, enno-bled beyond hate, violence and prejudice, yet not without passion.'

In 1930, the Huxleys settled in Sanary-sur-Mer in the South of France. This was to be their home base for the next seven years, where Aldous wrote his chilling view of the future, *Brave New World*, and also *Eyeless in Gaza*, a highly emotional inves-tigation and re-evaluation of his past. The prog-ress of the hero, Anthony Beavis, from misan-thropic cynicism to compassion for fellow men mirrors Huxley's own. With the rise of fascism in Europe, Huxley advocated in this book 'positive

High Society
By early 1932, the Huxleys were society figures – front page news for The Tatler. *Huxley, not yet 40, had already made his name with* Point Counter Point *and numerous stories and novels which had appeared almost annually since 1920. He was to lose popularity, however, with his decision to oppose the fascist threat with pacifism.*

By kind permission of Matthew Huxley

The TATLER

MR. AND MRS. ALDOUS HUXLEY AND THEIR SON

Illustrated London News

Eminent brothers
(left) Julian Huxley, as famous and respected a biologist as Aldous was a man of letters, cherished his meetings with his brother: 'From these encounters, I always returned to my work stimulated and refreshed, my spiritual batteries recharged.'

Impressions of India
(right) In 1925 Huxley saw Indian religion as an evil, commenting: "A little less spirituality, and the Indians would now be free . . . There would be less dirt and more food." Thirty years later, however, he embraced Hindu mysticism, becoming a devotee of Swami Prabhavananda in California.

Hollywood attractions
(below) The glamorous Coconut Grove in Hollywood attracted the stars and satellites of the film industry. And here Huxley benefited from lucrative commissions for film scripts – as well as the space and sunshine of California. Among his new friends were Charlie Chaplin, his actress wife Paulette Goddard, and the writer Anita Loos.

pacifism', an attempt to fill the prevailing moral vacuum of scepticism and negativity. But the British public were disenchanted by the didactic tone of *Eyeless in Gaza*; and Huxley's pacifism attracted criticism, as did his subsequent departure for the sunshine of California in April 1937.

His reasons for staying in the United States were complex, bound up with his physical and mental state, and the lure of 'easy money' as a Hollywood scriptwriter. Early in 1938, he was hospitalized with bronchitis; full recovery took over a year. He began intensive training in the Bates method, a series of exercises designed to improve eyesight, celebrating the results in *The Art of Seeing*. He also became seriously interested in Indian mysticism, seeking, perhaps, some inner peace at a time when the world was at war.

Later in 1939 Huxley successfully completed

THE COCOANUT GROVE,
AMBASSADOR HOTEL, LOS ANGELES.

his first script for MGM – an adaptation of *Pride and Prejudice* – and was fitfully employed by Hollywood throughout the 1940s, working on *Alice in Wonderland* and on an adaptation of his own short story *The Gioconda Smile* (released in 1948 as *A Woman's Vengeance*). He also investigated spiritualism and homeopathic medicine – the latter a consuming interest since the mid-Thirties, when he had studied with F. M. Alexander, founder of the Alexander Technique, a method of correcting defects in posture to improve mental and physical health. By May 1953, Huxley's researches had led him towards experimenting with hallucinogenic drugs (mescalin and later LSD) and his study of mescalin's mind-enlarging effects, *The Doors of Perception*, remains his most controversial work.

Two years later tragedy struck – Maria, who had done everything in her power to conceal her poor health from Aldous, died of a liver infec-

HUXLEY AND HALLUCINOGENS

In experimenting with psychedelic or hallucinogenic drugs – mescalin and LSD – Huxley was attempting to extend the frontiers of medical research. His aim was to study their effects on the consciousness. Drugs taken under the right circumstances (and by the right person) Huxley believed could be a force for social good, leading to a "sense of solidarity with the world and its spiritual principle". Although he was distressed by the misuse of drugs, he remained convinced that psychedelic drugs had the power to open doors in the mind that hitherto had been closed. He recorded his findings in the controversial *The Doors of Perception* (1954) and *Heaven and Hell* (1956).

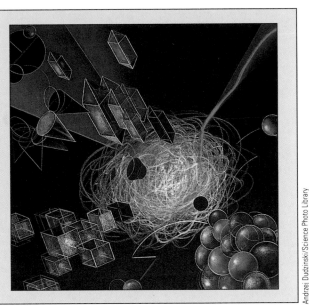

tion. Though friends and family worried that he would be totally helpless without her, Huxley soldiered on through his grief, and found consolation with a friend of his and Maria's, Laura Archera, 20 years his junior. She later recalled: 'I saw then, for the first time, how Aldous applied his philosophy: live here and now . . . He succeeded much of the time. Once in a while he would lapse into a depressed silence. He did not speak much about his pain; he only said, "It is like an amputation."'

The following year Aldous and Laura were quietly married at the Drive-in Wedding Chapel in Yuma, Arizona, on 19 March 1956. His new bride's youthful energy, determination and *joie de vivre* seemed to galvanize Aldous into a further bout of creative activity. He began a long-cherished project, a novel about the possibility of

Menuhin's accolade
To Yehudi Menuhin (below), Huxley was 'as pure in his maturity and ready to respond like a tuned violin in a trained hand'.

achieving an ideal society (later published as *Island*), re-examined the themes of *Brave New World* in *Brave New World Revisited* and then lectured in Italy.

In 1959, Huxley embarked on an academic career, becoming Visiting Professor at the University of California and delivering a course of lectures entitled *The Human Condition*. He also accepted an Award of Merit by the American Academy of Arts and Letters. Speedily recovering after treatment for a tumour on his tongue in 1960, he gave further lectures to packed auditoriums all over the US. Some recurrent themes – still relevant today – included the population explosion, human wastefulness with the earth's resources, and the evils of nationalism.

Amid this flurry of recognition by the American literary establishment and the plaudits of a new generation came a cruel blow – his house in Los Angeles was completely gutted by a bushfire. All his books and letters were destroyed. Huxley was soon back at work, however, writing, travelling and lecturing. In June 1962 he at last received acknowledgment of his achievements in Britain, and was elected Companion of Literature by the Royal Society of Literature.

THE FINAL TRAGEDY

A year later in September, tragedy struck for the last time in his life – a malignant tumour was discovered on his neck. He died on 22 November in Los Angeles; eight years later his ashes were returned to England and buried in his parents' grave at Compton in Surrey. Maria Huxley's ashes made the same journey in 1972.

Huxley's novels and essays remain the fascinating creations of one of this century's greatest 'pragmatic dreamers'. As Yehudi Menuhin wrote: 'This was a man in whom wisdom never destroyed innocence. He was a scientist and artist in one – standing for all we most need in a fragmented world . . .'

BRAVE NEW WORLD

In the perfectly controlled world of AF632, happiness is assured for all – it is sterile, indulged, permissive, safe. Here feelings of longing, fear, regret and doubt are seen as anarchic and aberrant.

It is not easy to be simultaneously funny and frightening about the future, but this is precisely what Aldous Huxley accomplishes in *Brave New World,* one of the undisputed classics of science fiction. Its humour resides in Huxley's satirical characterization of a futuristic Utopia, in which harmony and happiness flourish at the expense of truth and nature, and where humanity ranges below hygiene in the scale of State values.

The novel's ominousness comes from Huxley's conception of the future as an intensification of tendencies already present in modern society – notably the potential of science, machinery and technology for undermining the uniqueness of the individual and for diminishing the value, if not the quality, of life. The novel throughout walks a tightrope between humour and horror: it is a satire that ends in death.

GUIDE TO THE PLOT

The setting is London and the year is 632 AF (After Ford). As the Director of Hatcheries and Conditioning gives his guided tour around the centre to his new students, the reader is introduced to the concepts that underpin the functioning of Huxley's future world: a world of absolute stability and total sterility. Life is now created in the lab and such words as 'mother', 'parent' and 'family' are regarded not only as scientifically archaic but decidedly smutty. In this new world,

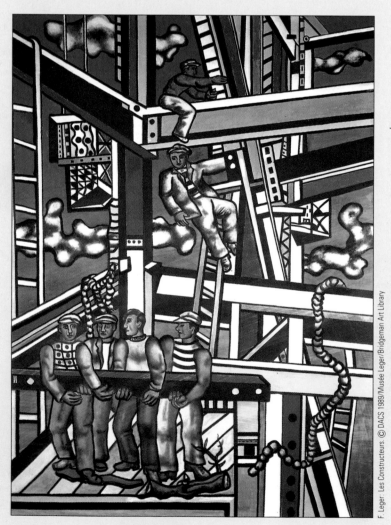

F. Leger: Les Constructeurs. © DACS 1989/Musée Leger/Bridgeman Art Library

Social order
"Everyone belongs to everyone else." So says the sleep-taught proverb. For the Alpha citizens it means a life full of frenetic activity, plentiful entertainment and sexual games. The lowest social order – the Epsilons (left) – carry out the essential manual labour that maintains the economy and services the brilliantly lit, scintillating world of their betters (above right). In return, they have their soma *ration, their sense of belonging and the security of knowing their place in the order of things.*

writer-lecturer Helmholtz Watson, who also has a vague feeling of frustration about his existence. "What the two men shared", says Huxley, "was the knowledge that they were individuals". This runs counter to one of the planet's main philosophical principles: "When the individual feels, the community reels." The two men are not outspoken enough to pose a threat to the society but they do exemplify a chink of imperfection.

A real threat, however, is on the horizon. When Bernard takes Lenina on a visit to a reservation in New Mexico (peopled by savages who have not been assimilated into the new world and who are still coping with such quaint problems as infirmity, squalor and monogamy), he is astonished to discover that one of the savages, John, is not only articulate but in fact shares some of Bernard's own feelings of sensitive alienation. His fascination increases when he deduces that the Savage is actually the Director's son, the unlikely product of a brief liaison long ago between the Director and John's mother, Linda, who had been lost on a visit to the

Feelies and flying
(above) Synthetic music, a scent organ and tactile special effects accompany the pornographic feelies' film showing at the Alhambra. Titillation "amid a blare of sexaphones" creates the sensations of orgiastic togetherness. But when Lenina takes John Savage to encounter the feelies, he finds them "base, ignoble". Lenina experiences a similar revulsion flying over the sea. Its untamed chaos fills her with disgust, and she is glad enough when the helicopter comes in to land among the artificial lights of 'civilisation' (left).

babies are not 'born' – they are decanted. All are allocated their place in society and are conditioned to "like their unescapable social destiny", which, the Director says, is "the secret of happiness and virtue".

The values of the State are not imposed by force but inculcated by sleep-teaching, or hypnopaedia. From an early age, the masses are conditioned to hate books and flowers. "A love of nature keeps no factories busy." Another teaching is that "everyone belongs to everyone else", which means that promiscuity is not only rampant but expected. Our Ford (like Henry Ford before him) has also decreed that "History is bunk", so that the past and even the ageing process have been eliminated. Furthermore, the drug *soma* is on hand to keep everyone fit and cheerful – or at least in a quasi-coma of unquestioning contentedness.

However, as is the convention in this kind of fiction, this 'perfect society' is not foolproof. Possibly because some alcohol leaked into his blood-surrogate, a young man from the Psychological Bureau, Bernard Marx is discontented. He has developed peculiarities of character that match an appearance less handsome than his Alpha-plus status warrants. He despises the entertainments of the masses and loves nature. Also his undisclosed feelings for the nurse Lenina Crowne are disturbingly akin to heartfelt love and not hearty lust. His only genuine friend is the

> *"The optimum population," said Mustapha Mond, "is modelled on the iceberg – eight-ninths below the water line, one-ninth above."*
> *"And they're happy below the water line?"*
> *"Happier than above it."*

reservation and is now a broken woman, ravaged by age and alcohol. On an impulse, Bernard invites John and Linda back to London. Enchanted by Lenina and excited at the prospect of meeting others like her, John exultantly quotes from Shakespeare's *The Tempest*: "O brave new world that has such people in it." But Bernard injects scepticism: "Hadn't you better wait until you actually see the new world?"

The impact of their arrival in the 'new world' is enormous. The revelation of their relationship with the Director compels the latter to resign, and John and Linda become the talk of upper-caste London, which in turn lifts Bernard to a new level of social esteem as the keeper of the Savage. However, it soon becomes clear that John is appalled by what he sees. When he starts to act on his revulsion, it is clearly time for the Controller, Mustapha Mond, to step in . . .

When *Brave New World* first appeared in

85

O BRAVE NEW WORLD!

The title comes from Shakespeare's play *The Tempest* (right), in which Miranda, totally innocent about the outside world, rejoices in her first glimpse of it. There are other parallels: Ariel the enslaved Alpha-plus, Caliban the brutalized Epsilon, and Prospero the paternalistic, autocratic manipulator who, like Mond, means well but oversteps human jurisdiction.

Robert Payton Reid: The Tempest/Fine Art Photographic Library

Monitor and recognizable names such as the Charing Cross Tower, which becomes the Charing-T Tower (Christian crosses are out, Ford's Model T is in).

SHIVERS OF PREMONITION
At the same time Huxley has fun with background details that seem comically absurd – the 'feelies', the synthetic music, the nursery rhymes for children ('Bye, Baby Banting, soon you'll be decanting') – and yet are more often than not sufficiently close to the reader's experience to cause a shiver of premonition. Sometimes the humour is a little heavy-handed and it has led to accusations of facetiousness. Yet Huxley is writing about a frivolous and superficial society and preparing the ground for a more savage second half where he can catch the reader off guard.

Another aspect of the novel's appeal is that, like most of Huxley's earlier work, it is very erotic. With great dash and finesse, Huxley is writing about a society that has basically found a philosophical justification for licentiousness. Although the point Huxley is making is a serious one – about the hollowness of hedonism – he is canny enough to exact the maximum eroticism out of the 'zip!' sound of Lenina's zippers as she disrobes in preparation for a sexual encounter.

Lenina's name – as with some others such as Bernard Marx and Polly Trotsky – is obviously significant. It might appear that the society Huxley is describing in *Brave New World* is intended to parody the Soviet system after the Revolution. Yet

1932, it was an immediate success, not only because of the originality of its ideas but because of its exuberant style. The message might be morbid, but Huxley knew how to entertain. For a long time the novel's seriousness – morally as well as philosophically – is disguised by the novelist's linguistic dexterity. He achieves a technical *tour-de-force* in Chapter Three, where he crosscuts nonchalantly between half a dozen different conversations taking place simultaneously. He plays around with catchphrases, updating them for the new society (e.g. "cleanliness is next to fordliness"), and he modifies the titles of reputable publications – the *Christian Science Monitor* becomes the *Fordian Science*

Savage culture
(left) The Indians on the reservation are the products of birth, marriage, religion, disease and an uncontrolled environment. To Lenina they are ugliness personified, but they possess something Bernard dimly covets.

Another wilderness
As disturbing influences, Bernard and Helmholtz are threatened with exile. Helmholtz chooses Iceland in the hope "one would write better if the climate were bad".

Victoria & Albert Museum/Bridgeman Art Library

Andrej Dudzinski/Science Photo Library

Huxley wrote the novel after a visit to the United States; and his description of Los Angeles at this time was 'the City of Dreadful Joy' – precisely what the planet is in *Brave New World;* and of course it is Our Ford who has replaced Our Lord. Unlike George Orwell and others, Huxley did not see the main threat to individual freedom as coming from totalitarianism. Rather, he saw it as a universal danger in all industrial societies

> "I don't want comfort… I want God, I want poetry, I want real dangers, I want freedom, I want goodness. I want sin."

Excesses
John's desire for Lenina is a confusion of passion and worship. Hers for him is all too quick, willing and unrepressed (right). The extremes of Lenina's voluptuousness and John's masochistic puritanism are equally perverse.

Delphin Enjolras: A Seductive Pose/Fine Art Photographic Library

which are dependent on consumerism and materialism.

This is the basis of the ideological debate between Mustapha Mond and the Savage that dominates the latter part of the novel. It is a stable and comfortable society, says the Controller, in which people have been programmed into accepting their roles and do not miss freedom because they are happy without it. It is a brainwashed society without soul, argues John, with a utilitarian attitude to

Out in the open
John Savage finds sanctuary in the country (below), but his novelty value is too great for him to be left in peace.

personality and with individuals on an assembly line of conformity. The main theme of *Brave New World,* according to Huxley, was 'the advancement of society as it affects human individuals'. His main image of that was the test-tube baby: 'no other symbol of the triumph of science over nature is anything like as effective as this', he said (one can imagine how Huxley might have felt about recent developments in this field). His main fear was that the development of science and technology would not only diminish individual freedom but also eventually sacrifice art, and that progress would develop inexorably into a depersonalized nightmare – what the intellectual Max

Eastman in 1922 foresaw as a 'modern world of capitalism and Communism . . . all rushing towards some enormous efficient machine-made doom of the true values of life'.

Whether the Savage is an effective mouthpiece for Huxley's fears is perhaps a debatable point. He is somewhat obsessed with the works of Shakespeare, and his sexual puritanism seems hardly less bizarre and abnormal than the society's sexual promiscuity. Yet the underlying validity of Huxley's vision can be felt in the influence it has had on other artists – from Charlie Chaplin's comic portrait of automated humanity in *Modern Times* (1936) to Anthony Burgess' similar debates about conditioning versus free will in *A Clockwork Orange* (1962).

A WORLD WITHOUT FEELING
It is perhaps Huxley's prescience about the atmosphere of modern society that is the most chillingly impressive aspect of the novel. We have our own *soma* nowadays – whether it be called advertising, television, consumerism – and the gods of efficiency, materialism and self-interest seem much more stridently assertive at the present time than those of spirituality and sensitivity. Huxley's cunning is to make his new world not overtly oppressive (as in George Orwell's *1984*), but superficially attractive, because it is clean, comfortable and without conflict or stress. Yet it is also a world without feeling and art – sterile, inert, impersonal. Who wants a 'brave new world', says Huxley, in which even the glorious poetry of Shakespeare falls on deaf ears? One could, of course, exist in such a world. One could not – in the fullest sense of the word – *live* in it.

Architectural Association/Peter Cook

PERCEPTIONS OF HELL

Despite his youthful, witty stance, Huxley's brief flame of optimism was extinguished by the certainty of pending destruction; he wrote with the urgency of despair.

'My health begins to break down as soon as I stop working', Aldous Huxley once said. His 40-odd volumes of novels, short stories, essays, travel writing, poetry, history, biography, plays and film scripts were packed with observations, information on an extraordinary range of subjects, and an unending stream of lively reflections and fresh ideas. For several decades he was generally admired – and cordially disliked by some – as the British intellectual *par excellence*, a man who made not the slightest effort to conceal his sharp mind and dauntingly vast knowledge.

Huxley was sometimes accused of 'literary over-production', mainly because he was known to have signed a series of three-year contracts with his publishers that obliged him to deliver two books every year from 1923 onwards. These contracts, however, ensured the financial security that enabled Huxley to function as a full-time author, freed at a relatively early age from seeking employment in journalism or teaching, as most other writers were driven to do in order to make a living. With all this creative activity, Huxley was certainly not a careless writer. As he himself put it, with characteristic wit, 'Generally I write everything many times over. All my thoughts are second thoughts.'

After publishing several books of poetry, Huxley emerged in the 1920s as a

Cecil Beaton/Courtesy of Sotheby's, London

Mark Gertler: The Pond at Garsington. Leeds Art Galleries

Angle of vision
Cecil Beaton chose to picture his celebrated subject (above) quizzically peering at the world from a detached view-point.

Literary haunt
The young Huxley was a frequent guest at Garsington Manor (left), the Oxfordshire home of Lady Ottoline Morrell, hostess to leading literary and political figures. This milieu fired his enthusiasm to write seriously.

brilliant satirist with three novels, *Crome Yellow* (1921), *Antic Hay* (1923) and *Those Barren Leaves* (1925). These, buttressed by the collections of short stories, essays and travel notes that appeared during the same period *(Limbo, Mortal Coils, On the Margin, Little Mexican, Along the Road)*, established Huxley as a prominent literary figure in an astonishingly short time. Many years later, Evelyn Waugh remembered *Antic Hay* with nostalgia as 'frivolous and sentimental and perennially delightful'; he and other writers were to follow Huxley's lead, making the 1920s a golden age of social comedy and satire.

As with most of Huxley's other works, these early novels abound in ideas about the past, present and future, but the ideas were played with so deftly and lightly that readers understandably identified the author with the gilded youth of post-war England, light-hearted even in its cynicism. *Crome Yellow,* for example, contained much that anticipated *Brave New*

Indian influence
(left) Huxley studied Indian mysticism as part of his search for meaning in life – an interest reflected in his later work.

Early success
Huxley published both poetry and prose while he was in his early twenties. His first book (right) – a collection of poems – came out soon after he left university.

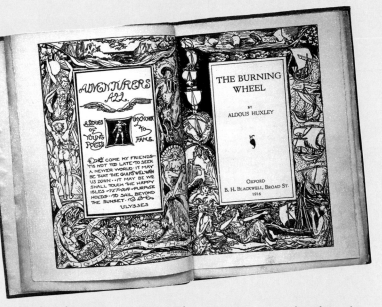

and should be maintained"; but he was also certain that their outward forms – for example, existing religious institutions – were completely dead and basically redundant. Over the next few years Huxley's ultimate concern – the search for spiritual enlightenment – became increasingly apparent.

Point Counter Point (1928), Huxley's longest and in many respects his most ambitious book, was still written in the form of a satire, and scored an even greater commercial success than the earlier novels; it was described by one critic as 'the modern *Vanity Fair*'. But Huxley's version had become significantly gloomier, and there was now no mistaking the depravity and violence of an increasingly complex contemporary

society. The message was echoed in the sophisticated structure of the book, in which characters and episodes were arranged in a pattern of parallels and contrasts, after the fashion of musical counterpoint. One of the characters, Philip Quarles, a novelist of ideas who feels cut off from emotional contact with others, was to some extent a self-portrait.

Like most novelists, Huxley based his characters on actual people; unlike most novelists, he admitted as much ('Of course I base my characters partly on

Meeting of minds
Huxley and D. H. Lawrence, two of the most stimulating and provocative writers of their time, were close friends and devotees of each other's work.

World, but it was far from clear at this stage of his writing that Huxley himself disapproved of the vision of "vast state incubators", foreseen by Scogan, in which "rows upon rows of gravid bottles will supply the world with the population it requires". Scogan discourses eloquently on the consequent dissociation of love from propagation: "Eros, beautifully and irresponsibly free, will flit like a gay butterfly from flower to flower through a sunlit world." But when another character remarks that this sounds lovely, Scogan drily comments that "The distant future always does."

However, readers of Huxley's non-fiction were already aware that he was in fact appalled by the spiritual emptiness of the modern world, and that he did not regard technological progress as a miracle cure to the problem. His travels round the world led him to the conclusion, voiced in *Jesting Pilate* (1926), that "the established spiritual values are fundamentally correct

91

people I know – one can't escape it'), although he argued that fictional human beings are always far less complex than real ones. The only positive characters in *Point Counter Point* are Mark and Mary Rampion, who were based on D. H. Lawrence and his wife Frieda. Rampion echoes Lawrence's belief in the 'blood knowledge' which he felt primitive cultures still possessed, and his insistence that the body must be given its due if the mind and spirit were to remain healthy. 'To be a perfect animal *and* a perfect human – that was the ideal', according to Rampion. Ironically, Lawrence scornfully dismissed the character as 'a gas-bag'.

Huxley soon shook off the influence of Lawrence's primitivism, although a trace may have survived in his choice of a Red Indian protagonist for *Brave New World* (1932). 'A comic book – but seriously comic', this novel was begun 'as a parody of H. G. Wells' *Men Like Gods,* but gradually . . . got out of hand and turned into something quite different'. Readers immediately realized that *Brave New World* had the durable quality of a classic, and although Huxley's reputation has fluctuated widely over the years, this alone of all his books has never fallen from favour or gone out of print.

A RADICAL CHANGE

During the early 1930s Huxley's fame was at its height; and it was at this point that his work underwent a radical change. Although he continued to play the satirist from time to time, he became increasingly concerned to find solutions to the world's ailments. Ever since, Huxley's admirers seem to have fallen into two opposing camps. One group admires the satirical novels and believes that Huxley committed artistic suicide by introducing long essays on pacifism and mysticism into his later works; the other group views these as the natural development and fulfilment of Huxley's earlier ideas and observations.

Huxley himself was aware that, as a 'novelist of ideas', he was likely to be suspected of a lack of interest in ordinary human beings or, alternatively, of a lack of reverence for the novel as a close-crafted art form in the tradition of Henry James. And on occasion he did admit to not being 'a congenital novelist', to finding it difficult, for example, to invent plots. But he also believed that the highest kind of art was not the spare, 'pure' work, but one that included as much of the untidy stuff of reality as possible – 'the lively, the mixed and the incomplete'. And that 'Other things being equal, the work of art which in its own way "says"

more about the universe will be better than the work of art which says less.' If fiction could help men and women to understand reality and improve their lives, so much the better. For all his intellectuality, Huxley was far from being an ivory-tower novelist.

Ever sensitive to contemporary developments, Huxley signalled his change of direction with a book that confronted the problems raised by the menace of fascism in the 1930s. *Eyeless in Gaza* (1936) and non-fiction works such as *Ends and Means* (1937) courageously advocated outright pacifism, on the grounds that evil means – violence – can only lead to evil results. *Eyeless in Gaza* also marks the beginning of Huxley's obsession with the conquest of time, its

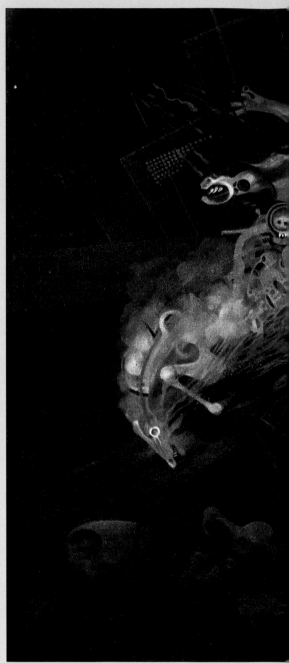

episodes 'shifting back and forth in time to show the pressure of the past on the present'.

Huxley's conviction that only a mystical or religious path could 'cure' modern man was expressed most clearly in the novels *After Many a Summer* (1939) and the significantly titled *Time Must Have a Stop* (1944). In the former, the mystic character William Propter argues that "Actual good is outside time", that is, in eternity. *The Perennial Philosophy*

Hollywood scriptwriter
An extremely versatile writer, Huxley earned in excess of $1500 a week writing film scripts. His adaptation of Jane Austen's Pride and Prejudice *became a star-studded success.*

each individual to save him- or herself, abandoning any possibility of improving human life by means of action, which is necessarily time-bound. In practice, however, he remained very much involved in human affairs. Two widely-praised historical studies, *Grey Eminence* (1941) and *The Devils of Loudun* (1952), examined the tragic incompatibility between religious convictions and the exercise of power. And the development and use of the atomic bomb prompted Huxley to project a vision of the future very different from that of *Brave New World*. Long before such predictions became fashionable, *Ape and Essence* (1948) pictures a post-holocaust California where the radiation-damaged inhabitants have been enslaved by the fanatical priests of a diabolical religion, and human culture has been destroyed. At this point cemeteries are plundered for jewellery and other arte-facts, as no-one is now sufficiently skilled to produce such objects. More soberly, the essays collected in *Brave New World Revisited* (1958) dealt with the looming threats to human freedom: ecological, scientific and organizational.

MYSTICAL EXPERIENCES

Much more of a sensation was caused by Huxley's advocacy of the drugs mescalin and LSD as short cuts to mystical experience. In *The Doors of Perception* (1954) and *Heaven and Hell* (1956) he described the extraordinary effects of those hallucinogenic drugs, claiming that they were 'physiologically innocuous' and helped people to look at the world in a new way. These writings made Huxley one of the gurus of a new generation. But not everyone was impressed: the famous German novelist Thomas Mann remarked sourly of Huxley that 'meditating over the awesome existence of a chair and on various delightful colour illusions has more to do with stupidity than he thinks'. Even at the moment of his death, Huxley was still seeking to enlarge his perceptions by the use of LSD.

In his last novel, *Island* (1962), Huxley returned yet again to the subject of Utopia. This time he tried to imagine the good society – one in which the useful aspects of technology and modern civilization (including contraception and drugs) could be incorporated into a way of life blending the wisdom and skills of East and West to produce sane, balanced human beings. Although not entirely successful as a novel, it made a valuable contribution to Huxley's life-work for its typically brilliant, provocative and future-piercing ideas.

Psychedelia
(above) Huxley's experimentation with hallucinogenic drugs plunged him into controversy. He put his visionary experiences into a long essay, Heaven and Hell.

Man of letters
(right) Gaunt and bespectacled, Huxley appeared stereotypically bookish. But in reality he was constantly tackling contemporary and avant-garde issues.

(1945), part-anthology, part-commentary, brought together the common elements in most of the world's great religions, providing an influential 'bible' for the spiritually perplexed.

In *After Many a Summer* Huxley appeared to be preaching the necessity for

Aldous Huxley's literary career was a remarkable spiritual odyssey that turned him from a daring 1920s wit into a mystic and guru of the 1960s. In *Crome Yellow* (1921), the foibles of sophisticates are described with merciless satiric gusto. At first more amused than angry, Huxley's view grew strongly disapproving in *Point Counter Point* (1928), a large-scale portrait of London society. *Brave New World* (1932) projected the same concerns into the future. *Eyeless in Gaza* (1936) attempted a solution in the pacifism and moral commitment of the main character. But by 1939, in *After Many a Summer*, Huxley had abandoned schemes for human improvement and advocated the pursuit of mystical knowledge. Later writings such as *The Doors of Perception* (1954) see drugs as a short-cut to mystical experience; while his antidote to *Brave New World* is the balanced, fully human society of *Island* (1962).

Henry Gerbault: Palm Court (detail)/Fine Art Photographic Library

Mary Evans Picture Library

POINT COUNTER POINT

◆1928◆

Fated to be loved and left by frenetic good-time girl Lucy Tantamount (left), Walter Bidlake is a familiar Huxley character, weak and treacherous. Other unpleasant characters in this dark vision of London society include Evrard Webley, a fascist politician; Spandrell, whose hatred of life drives him to commit a motiveless murder; and novelist Philip Quarles who cannot relate to other people. He is impregnable in his isolation, even when his little son is dying. Artist Mark Rampion diagnoses the situation by painting grotesques. Sickness and savagery dominate the climax.

CROME YELLOW

◆1921◆

A house-party unites a group of hopeless, feckless young things (left). The poet Denis Stone arrives at Crome, country home of Priscilla Wimbush, whose passions are the occult and gambling. Her husband Henry is absorbed in his *History of Crome*. Other guests include Anne, with whom Denis is irresolutely in love; 'modern', moon-faced Mary Bracegirdle; and the Byronic Gombauld. Mary, determined not to be a prey to Freudian repressions, has her first affair — and finds she might have been better off repressed. And Denis, tortured by jealousy, makes his first real decision, an instantly disastrous one.

Andrzej Dudzinski/Science Photo Library

EYELESS IN GAZA
━◆ 1936 ◆━

Casual love affairs, with no basis in genuine feeling (below) are symptomatic of Anthony Beavis' inability to relate deeply to other people. His childhood and schooldays have rendered him an insular intellectual; his worst sin is the seduction of his best friend's fiancée, resulting in the friend's suicide. Even so, there is hope for Anthony: he learns from his past. And when he goes to Mexico, intending to take part in a violent revolution, he meets a man who gives his life an extraordinary new direction.

Warne Bros/Kobal Collection

Thomas Hart Benton: City Activities (detail). Courtesy of the Equitable

THE DEVILS OF LOUDUN
━◆ 1952 ◆━

An agonized death (above) is the consequence of uncontrolled sexual depravity, after a community of nuns succumbs to group hysteria. A phenomenon interpreted by medieval minds as possession by devils, this historical event is the subject of a scholarly study by Huxley. It formed the basis for John Whiting's play, *The Devils*, which was itself made into a film.

AFTER MANY A SUMMER
━◆ 1939 ◆━

Humanity's need to escape time (left), is one theme of this bizarre, didactic, mystical novel. But American millionaire Jo Stoyte is simply intent on escaping the ageing process. He employs the cynical Dr Obispo to this end and Obispo promptly helps himself to Stoyte's mistress. In a jealous rage, Stoyte murders the wrong man. Partly to evade justice, but more to pursue rumours of the rejuvenating properties of carp guts, Stoyte comes to England. There he meets a man who has indeed found immortality — but at what cost?

"FORDLINESS"

This farmboy-made-good seemed to promise a future full of affordable luxuries. But as time passed, Henry Ford showed another face to the people who had made him rich.

In Huxley's sterile Utopia of the future, his 'brave new world', the place of God is taken by the American car mogul Henry Ford. People swear by the name of Our Ford, and years are counted from the introduction of the Ford Model T motor car. "Ford's in his flivver", the happy people sigh, "All's well with the world." Huxley wrote in the early 1930s; he could see all too plainly the seeds of his disturbing vision of the future in the rise of the new consumer society, and deplored its materialism. Few people had done more to bring that society into existence and foster its values than Henry Ford.

Henry Ford himself was something of a hero to many ordinary American people, a man whose rags-to-riches success lay at the heart of the American dream. What he had done, any American with the will and the talent might do too. Ford seemed to have the interests of 'the little man' at heart, and his down-to-earth, no-nonsense personality appeared reassuring in a rapidly changing world. When Americans were polled in the 1920s about who they wanted as president, the carmaker from Detroit was far and away the most popular choice, even though he was never a candidate.

Yet Ford was a man of extraordinary contradictions. The Henry Ford who gave his workers the highest wages in America in 1914, was the same Ford who hounded and beat them to despair in the 1930s. The Ford who took on poor immigrants when no other employer would, was also the Ford who became fanatically anti-Jewish in the 1920s.

Rags to riches
A country lad from Michigan, Ford rose to be America's wealthiest industrialist. As pioneer of the world's first cheap car, of mass production and of high wages for shorter hours, he gained a dangerously heady power over the hearts and minds of the people. He had genius, but ultimately lacked wisdom.

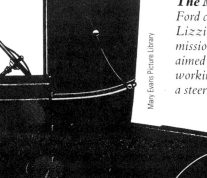

The Model T
Ford crusaded for the 'Tin Lizzie' (left) with missionary zeal. He aimed to put every hard-working American behind a steering wheel.

Assembly-line life

The assembly line made Ford a multi-millionaire. The first was built from 'railroad ties, iron slides, and some horses, and they pulled it with a rope'. By the time the Highland Park factory (right) was founded in Detroit in 1913, 'The Ford machinery was the best in the world, everybody knew it.' The assembly line so revolutionized car manufacture that it swiftly took over in Europe (below right) as well as the States. But workers hated it.

Mary Evans Picture Library

The General Utility Car

& RELIABLE

EVERYWHERE.

Victoria & Albert Museum/Bridgeman Art Library

Self-advertisement

Ford's belief in his Model T became so absolute that he cancelled advertisements like the one above, believing the car would sell itself. By every post he received letters from farmers enclosing photographs of the 'flivver' pulling ploughs, driving threshing machines, saws and vacuum cleaners, and taking bucolic families on week-end picnics. Why waste money on advertising?

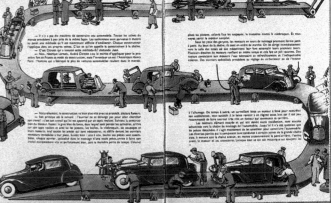

The Ford who campaigned for peace in the Great War let his factories be used to churn out arms only months later.

Before Ford came along, motor cars were regarded as rich men's toys, far too expensive and elaborate ever to become everyday means of transport. Ford's dream was to create a car so cheap that even those with modest incomes could afford to buy one.

'I will build a car for the multitude', he earnestly proclaimed. 'It will be large enough for the family but small enough for the individual to run and care for. It will be constructed of the best materials, by the best men to be hired, after the simplest designs that modern engineering can devise. But it will be so low in price that no man making a good salary will be unable to own one – and enjoy with his family the blessings of hours of pleasure in God's great open spaces.'

It was an idea he had cherished ever since he was a boy on his father's farm in Dearborn, Michigan, tinkering with clocks and home-made steam engines in the workshop. 'Hitch your wagon to a star', he had heard the preacher advise one day, and this was his wagon and his star. But for years he could not persuade any of his backers that the idea made business sense. The Ford Motor Company (formed in 1903 when he was 40), grew rich on sales of luxury cars. Ford managed to buy out the opposition with his share of the profits and set to work on his People's Car.

The Model T was created in a tiny room in the Ford Motor Company's Detroit factory. For a year, as the T came gradually to life, Henry Ford would sketch his ideas on a big blackboard, or sit in a rocking chair late into the night, watching the engineers build the car and discussing progress. Ford's little team were fired by his almost childlike enthusiasm. 'God, he could get anything out of us. He'd never say, "I want this done." He'd say, "I wonder if we can do this? I wonder?" Well the men would break their necks to see if they could do it.'

The Model T was finally launched in spring 1908 and its success almost exceeded even Ford's extravagant imagination. Nicknamed affectionately, 'Tin Lizzie' and the 'flivver', this light but rugged little car, perfect for the rough country roads of the day, captured the American imagination and was selling by the thousand within months of its launch. And where America led, Europe soon followed. Before long, Ford's only problem was meeting the enormous demand – and the fact that the price of the car, at over $800, was still much too high for his liking.

MASS PRODUCTION

Ford had argued for years that 'the way to make automobiles is . . . to make them come through the factory just alike, just as one pin is like another when it comes from a pin factory', and the success of the Lizzie gave him the chance to prove it. Standardization opened the way for mass production, and mass production could bring the lower prices Ford craved. Ford's approach was simple but revolutionary: cut prices and you sell more; sell more and you can improve efficiency by mass production, enabling you to cut prices again.

The Ford Company had already tried basic

Sources and Inspiration

mass production techniques, with teams of men pulling a part-assembled car through the factory on a rope, while other teams were adding on parts as it moved. Now they built a huge factory at Highland Park in Detroit unlike anything ever seen before.

The Highland Park plant, described by awed visitors as 'the crystal palace' because of its vast windows, was a marvel of organization, with four huge assembly floors, linked together by continuously moving lifts, chutes and conveyor belts, and equipped with some 15,000 specially-designed machines. In its first year of operation (1910), the plant turned out almost 20,000 Model Ts; in 1912 it produced almost four times that number. But Ford's greatest innovation was the assembly line.

'Time loves to be wasted', he often warned, and the assembly line cut wasted time to a minimum, assigning to every worker one simple task which he repeated endlessly and rapidly as components glided past on a moving belt. The acceleration in output was staggering, and in 1913, production of the Model T leaped from 78,000 to almost 250,000. Ford was able to cut the price of the T to $440, noting happily, 'Every time I reduce the charge for our car by one dollar, I get a thousand new buyers.'

But as the Ford company's sales soared to new heights, so the morale of its workers slumped. Henry Ford's personal wealth was huge, but his employees took home a pittance, and the new assembly line with its mindless repetition made them feel like automatons. Few workers could put up with it for more than a couple of months, and turnover of staff at the Highland Park was alarmingly swift.

The company's solution, suggested by Ford's partner James Couzens, was simple but dramatic. They would double average wages to $5 a day and cut the basic working day from 12 to eight hours, converting the factory from two to three shifts. It would be, they claimed, 'the greatest revolution in the matter of rewards for its workers ever known to the industrial world.'

The announcement created a furore, and almost overnight Henry Ford became the most famous industrialist in America. The New York *Globe* was full of praise, saying, 'It has all the advantages and none of the disadvantages of socialism', but the *Wall Street Journal* condemned it as a deeply immoral misapplication of Biblical principles.

Ford was tickled pink by his sudden fame. He had always wanted to be philosopher-inventor like his hero Thomas Edison, not just a rich industrialist, and for years had been jotting down his own pet sayings in little notebooks that he bought by the gross. Now at last he had his chance, and he was in his element casting pearls of wisdom to the eager press. The American public lapped it all up, and his frequent pronouncements on life were looked to almost as the words of a prophet. He won a reputation as a socialist, but his ideas were never more than skin deep.

A moralizing side had always been present in

THE **KEY** TO THE

MUNITIONS
MEN
AND
MONEY

ARE
YOU
HELPING
TO
TURN IT?

SITUATION

War efforts
Of World War I Ford said to the Press in an unguarded moment, 'I'd give all my money – and my life – to stop it.' The remark committed him to a public show of pacifism which his later manufacture of armaments (above) belied.

Out of step
Some thought it quaint that Ford should hark back to bygone joys (left), old-time dancing (above) and the innocence of a pre-industrial world. But a ruthless egomania accompanied his 'eccentricity', and little by little he fell out of step with family, workers and the modern world.

NA/Kobal Collection

Ford's apparently simple nature, and now it surfaced with a vengeance. He determined that his workers should not only be paid better, but that they should live better too; the Ford company would turn out better men the way they turned out better cars. So he made the $5 day dependent on a workman's sobriety, decency and self-reliance, and set up a force of company social workers to carry through his ideas.

Many Ford workers understandably resented the frequent intrusion of Ford's Sociological Department into their private lives, but put up with it for the sake of the wages. And there is no doubt that Ford helped the company take on workers that other employers would shun – ex-convicts and immigrants, for example. Firmly believing in the benefits of honest toil, Ford himself would often stop his car to pick up hitch-hikers and tramps to offer them a job at his factory – a chance to 'remake their lives'.

FIGHTING FOR PEACE

Ford developed an inspirational belief in his own ability to change the world. When the War in Europe, and America's potential involvement, threatened to ruin all he was working for, he chartered a ship to sail the Atlantic with a group of anti-War activists on a crusade for peace. New York intellectuals ridiculed him mercilessly, but the American public loved him for it. Then, in mid-ocean, Ford seemed to realize that while he was king in Detroit, he was out of his depth in world politics, and soon after the Peace Ship had docked in Europe he abandoned the project and slipped quietly back home.

Both those who dismissed Ford as a mere publicity-seeker and those who saw him as a simpleton were given ammunition by the speed with which his pacifist ideas evaporated. Soon after America had joined the War, Ford conceived a tank based on the Model T and a one-man submarine, nicknamed by journalists the 'U-flivver'.

Machine-age man
For all his paternalism, Henry Ford built factories on a principle of repetitive, unremitting labour which reduced workers to mere cogs in the production process. Chaplin's 1936 film Modern Times *(above) lampooned this dehumanizing aspect of the great Industrial Dream. It came out at a time when the Depression had turned Ford employees' unpleasant work into an intolerable, grinding slavery, without even the compensation of high wages. The film touched a raw nerve in Americans who had once hero-worshipped Ford and his imitators.*

Critics began to snipe at his regular press comments, and on 22 June 1916 the Chicago *Tribune* described him as too ignorant to make any pronouncements to the public at all. Ford immediately sued for libel.

At the trial three years later, Ford was taken apart by the defence lawyer, who argued that Ford was a fraud, too ill-informed to set himself up as an educator of the people. Ford, relying on his epigrams to see him through, was completely floored when the lawyer tested him on his education. During the trial he defined 'chilli con carne' as a large mobile army and 'ballyhoo' as a blackguard, and announced that the American Revolution was in 1812. At one stage he admitted candidly, 'I am ignorant about most things.' Ford won his case, but lost his reputation.

Chastened by the trial and by the failure of his Peace Mission, Ford began to turn inwards. It was as if the challenge of the modern world had become too much for him. From 1920, the cranky side of his nature, always present, began to come to the fore. A golden haze crept over his memories of the boyhood farm he had been so eager to leave, and he started to cherish the past in a way that seemed almost perverse in a man who had done so much to bring the world into the 20th century. Rural America was the real America, he felt: the America of his father, the America fast disappearing in the urbanized, consumerized, hectic world he had helped to create.

The Ford farm at Dearborn he lovingly preserved as it was when he was boy, and often took half-a-dozen boys out there to eat hickory nuts and jump from the hayrick just as he had done all those years ago. He also built up a vast and eccentric collection of artefacts of the real America – it was said that he had one of every kind of shoe ever made in America – and spent billions of dollars building a museum village to preserve the ways of the past. And, to combat the modern tendency for 'sex dancing', he made strenuous efforts to revive the old-time dances of his youth, hiring a dancing master to teach Ford employees how to 'gallop', and painting the steps on the floor of the Engineering Building to help them. None of his top executives dared to miss the weekly dances, where the spritely 60-year-old company head pulled them each in turn around the floor.

THINGS OF THE PAST

Ford's obsession with the past began to spill over into the Motor Company too. Even in 1920, the Tin Lizzie was looking antiquated next to the sleek, sophisticated cars emerging from General Motors and Chrysler. Yet six years later, Ford was still stubbornly resisting any attempts to develop a new Ford car, despite plummeting sales. 'The only thing wrong with that car', he insisted later, 'was that people stopped buying it'.

Some people dismissed all this as harmless eccentricity. But there was something dangerously xenophobic about his retreat into the values of middle America and, in the early 1920s, it

BBC Hulton Picture Library

Mary Evans Picture Library

Brakes full on

Ford's overweening confidence in his Model T became a serious stumbling-block in the Thirties. As an old man, nostalgic for the Good Old Days (he is pictured above in his very first car), he no longer saw the need for continual improvement. The joke attributed to him, 'You can have any colour so long as it's black,' summed up his dictatorial attitude towards his customers.

THE MORRIS ISIS SIX
SALOON From £385 ex-works
MORRIS MOTORS LTD. COWLEY. OXFORD

Overtaking

Competitors began bringing out chic, streamlined, stylish cars backed up by image-conscious advertising (above). They swept past the Model T in the outside lane, and left it looking primitive and outmoded. Deaf to the advice of his executives, Henry Ford held on to the reins far too long for the good of his empire.

emerged hideously in an outburst of fanatical anti-Semitism. Convinced that a naturally corrupt conspiracy of Jewish bankers was trying to enslave the honest working man, he hired researchers to find evidence for his belief, and set up a newspaper – which he insisted all Ford customers receive – to expound his views. It is hardly any wonder that in the 1920s Hitler had a picture of Ford on his desk.

FORD AND BENNETT

Ford abandoned his anti-Jewish crusade after losing a libel case, but the nickname of 'Crazy Henry', coined in the days when he was building his first car, began to ring ominously true. Ford had always possessed what people said was his 'mean streak', a livid vein of nastiness which showed itself in cruel practical jokes and, as he grew older, a ruthless obsessiveness.

He had certainly spared no-one in his struggle to achieve total control of the Ford Motor Company, making it by far the largest individually-owned company in the world. And once he was in sole command, Ford's despotic style of management slowly poisoned the positive atmosphere that had made Ford workers proud to be part of the company in better years. A witch-hunt slowly pushed out anyone who would not toe the Ford line, and morale slumped as sharply as sales of Ford cars.

In this cut-throat climate, it was the tough guys who won Ford's praise, and none was tougher than Harry Bennett, an Al Capone-like character whose connections with the gangster world of 1930s America were well-known. Ford doted on Bennett, who flattered him by carrying out even Ford's strangest whims ruthlessly. One day, driving past a Ford-owned garage, Ford asked timidly, 'Why are we in the gas business, Harry?' Later that day, Bennett showed Ford the garage again, now bulldozed flat and covered with turfs and little trees. 'That's nice, Harry', said Ford.

The Great Depression of the 1930s drove down wages throughout the industry and Ford workers suffered more than most. The good times of the $5 day were forgotten and the assembly line was accelerated. At Ford, the regimented nightmare pastiched in Charlie Chaplin's film *Modern Times* was a reality, and men collapsed out of exhaustion and despair: Detroit doctors called it 'Forditis'.

The workers were ripe for unionization but, on Ford's instructions, Bennett organized a huge army of hoods and toughs to carry out 'security' operations, spying on every member of the company in and outside work. Workers suspected of union sympathies were searched regularly for union literature, intimidated, dismissed or just beaten up. According to one account, 'There was no sitting, squatting, singing, talking or whistling on the job'. Smiling was frowned upon. Workers learned to communicate without moving their lips in what became known as the 'Ford whisper'.

As other motor car companies gradually gave way to the pressure for unionization, Ford held out tenaciously, encouraging Bennett's mobsters to increasingly violent tactics. When in 1937 pictures of bloodied union men and women, brutally beaten by Bennett's men, appeared, splashed across the newspapers, Ford's days as the 'man of the people' were over. Three years later, desperate Ford workers finally went out on strike. With machine guns mounted on the factory walls, Ford and Bennett were ready for a pitched battle, but at the last minute Ford's wife argued for peace.

Ford was now almost 80, irascible and unreasonable. He became more and more reclusive, spending days at a time alone with his wife in their big house at Fairlane. In 1943 his son Edsel died, harried to an early grave, many said, by Ford and Bennett because he had tried to fight his father's worst excesses. Ford was distraught with grief and guilt, consoling himself with his belief in reincarnation, but it was not enough. In 1947 he died a frail, unhappy, lonely old man.

BIBLIOGRAPHY

Bedford, Sybille, *Aldous Huxley*. Carroll & Graf (New York, 1985)

Bloom, Harold, intro. by, *Lewis Carroll*. Chelsea House (New York, 1987)

Bogart, Max, ed., *The Jazz Age*. Macmillan (New York, 1969)

Chakoo, B. L., *Aldous Huxley and Eastern Wisdom*. Humanities Press International (Atlantic Highlands, 1981)

Childs, John, *The Army, James II and the Glorious Revolution*. St. Martin's Press (New York, 1981)

Chisholm, Anne, *Nancy Cunard: A Biography*. Penguin Books (New York, 1981)

Collier, Peter, and Horowitz, David, *The Fords: An American Epic*. Summit Books (New York, 1988)

Collins, John C., *Jonathan Swift: A Biographical and Critical Study*. Folcroft (Folcroft, 1983)

Crabbe, Katharyn W., *Evelyn Waugh*. Ungar Publishing (New York, 1988)

De Rios, Marlene D., *Hallucinogens: Cross-Cultural Perspectives*. University of New Mexico Press (Albuquerque, 1984)

Downie, J. A., *Jonathan Swift: Political Writer*. Routledge, Chapman & Hall (New York, 1986)

Ferns, C. S., *Aldous Huxley: Novelist*. Humanities Press International (Atlantic Highlands, 1980)

Firchow, Peter E., *The End of Utopia: A Study of Aldous Huxley's Brave New World*. Bucknell University Press (Cranbury, 1984)

Frost, William, *John Dryden: Dramatist, Satirist, Translator*. AMS Press (New York, 1988)

Gay, Phoebe F., *John Gay: His Place in the Eighteenth Century* (reprint of 1938 edition). Richard West (Philadelphia, 1973)

Gernsheim, Helmut, *Lewis Carroll: Photographer*. Dover Publications (New York, 1970)

Guiliano, Edward, and Kincaid, James R., eds., *Soaring with the Dodo: Essays on Lewis Carroll's Life and Art*. University Press of Virginia (Charlottesville, 1982)

Heath, Jeffrey M., *The Picturesque Prison: Evelyn Waugh and His Writing*. McGill-Queens University Press (Cheektowaga, 1982)

Hudson, Derek, *Lewis Carroll* (reprint of 1954 edition). Greenwood Press (Westport, 1972)

Hunting, Robert, *Jonathan Swift*. G. K. Hall (Boston, 1967)

Huxley, Aldous, *The Basic Philosophy of Aldous Huxley*. American Institute for Psychological Research (Albuquerque, 1984)

Jackson, Robert W., *Jonathan Swift: Dean and Pastor* (reprint of 1939 edition). Richard West (Philadelphia, 1980)

Kelly, Richard, *Lewis Carroll*. G. K. Hall (Boston, 1977)

Lane, Calvin W., *Evelyn Waugh*. G. K. Hall (Boston, 1981)

Leighton, Gerald, *Huxley: His Life and Work*. Richard West (Philadelphia, 1980)

Lemagny, Jean-Claude, and Rouille, Andre, eds., *A History of Photography: Social and Cultural Perspectives*. Cambridge University Press (New York, 1987)

Maas, Jeremy, *Holman Hunt and the Light of the World*. Gower Publishing (Brookfield, 1987)

Mack, Maynard, *Alexander Pope: A Life*. Yale University Press (New Haven, 1985)

McCartney, George, *Confused Roaring: Evelyn Waugh and the Modernist Tradition*. Indiana University Press (Bloomington, 1987)

McDonnell, Jacqueline, *Waugh on Women*. St. Martin's Press (New York, 1986)

Nye, David E., *Henry Ford: Ignorant Idealist*. Associated Faculty Press (New York, 1979)

Ovendon, Graham, ed., *A Victorian Album: Julia Margaret Cameron and Her Circle*. Da Capo Press (Jersey City, 1975)

Pudney, John, *Lewis Carroll and His World*. Scribner's (New York, 1976)

Robb, David, *George MacDonald*. Longwood Publishing (Wolfeboro, 1987)

Rosenheim, Edward W., Jr., *Swift and the Satirist's Art*. University of Chicago Press (Chicago, 1982)

Stern, Jeffrey, ed., *Lewis Carroll's Library*. Lewis Carroll Society of North America (Silver Spring, 1981)

Wolff, L., *Dante Gabriel Rossetti*. Richard West (Philadelphia, 1973)

Wood, Douglas K., *Men Against Time: Nicolas Berdyaev, T. S. Eliot, Aldous Huxley and C. G. Jung*. University Press of Kansas (Lawrence, 1982)

INDEX